Linguistic Development through

POETRY MEMORIZATION

Student Book

by Andrew Pudewa

illustrated by Anthea Segger

Second Edition, February 2016
Institute for Excellence in Writing, L.L.C.

Also by Andrew Pudewa

Advanced Communication Series
Advanced Spelling and Vocabulary
Bible-Based Writing Lessons
Phonetic Zoo Spelling Program (Levels A, B, and C)
The Profound Effects of Music on Life
Speech Boot Camp
Student Writing Intensive (Levels A, B, and C)
Student Intensive Continuation Course (Levels A, B, and C)
Teaching Writing: Structure and Style
The Two Andrews: On Writing and Teaching Writing

Copyright Policy

Linguistic Development through Poetry Memorization
Second Edition, February 2016

ISBN: 978-1-62341-260-9

Institute for Excellence in Writing
8799 N. 387 Road
Locust Grove, OK 74352
800.856.5815

info@IEW.com
IEW.com

Printed in the United States of America

Acknowledgments

Many thanks to all who assisted in the concept and creation of this program, especially:

Harold Pudewa and Marcia McCarry, whose excellent parenting gave me a love for poetry and aptitude with language, enabling me to do the work I do today.

My wife, Robin Pudewa, and all my children, whose enthusiasm for this project gave me the confidence and energy to see it to completion.

Maria Gerber, Julie Marie Ash, Lori Brians, Peter Buscemi, Genevieve Pudewa Priest, and several others, whose research, input, and careful editing contributed greatly to the finished product.

Jill Pike, author of IEW's *Primary Arts of Language* (PAL) and a personal friend, who contributed tremendously to this Second Edition with speech annotations and lesson enhancements.

Michael Rabb, a talented homeschooled musician, who graciously provided the piano chimes for the audio recordings.

The many teachers, parents, and students who listened in seminars and lectures as I worked out the concept for this program.

Contents

Level One

Poems

Getting Started with Level One

1. Begin with the first poem, "Ooey Gooey."
2. Highlight the poem in the list below.
3. Practice daily. Use the audio recording to help you.
4. Continue to memorize the poetry in the list, poem by poem. Work at your own pace.
5. Every day, recite all the poems you have learned. That is what the highlighting is for: Recite the highlighted poems daily. Use the recording to help you.
6. Record your progress on the chart below. A check for the day means that you recited all the poems that you have highlighted.

> Practice all the poems learned every day.
>
> Recite the name and author with the poem.
>
> Break longer poems into sections and memorize one section at a time.
>
> If you miss a day, do not try to do double the work. Just pick it up where you left off, and determine to be faithful to the task.

1 **Ooey Gooey** author unknown
2 **Celery** by Ogden Nash
3 **The Little Man Who Wasn't There** by Hughes Mearns
4 **The Vulture** by Hilaire Belloc
5 **After the Party** by William Wise
6 **Singing Time** by Rose Fyleman
7 **The Yak** by Hilaire Belloc
8 **The Ingenious Little Old Man** by John Bennett
9 **My Shadow** by Robert Louis Stevenson
10 **There Was an Old Person Whose Habits** by Edward Lear
11 **Jonathan Bing** by Beatrice Curtis Brown
12 **Whole Duty of Children** by Robert Louis Stevenson
13 **Godfrey Gordon Gustavus Gore** by William Brighty Rands
14 **My Gift** by Christina Rossetti
15 **The Swing** by Robert Louis Stevenson
16 **Persevere** author unknown
17 **Who Has Seen the Wind?** by Christina Rossetti
18 **The Eagle** by Alfred, Lord Tennyson
19 **The Swan and the Goose** by William Ellery Leonard
20 **Personal selection** (8 lines or shorter):

____

Below, check off the day when you have recited all of the poems you have learned to date.

	1	2	3	4	5	6	7	8	9	10	11	12	13	14	15	16	17	18	19	20	21	22	23	24	25	26	27	28	29	30	31
Aug																															
Sep																															
Oct																															
Nov																															
Dec																															
Jan																															
Feb																															
Mar																															
Apr																															
May																															
Jun																															
Jul																															

1.
Ooey Gooey

AUTHOR UNKNOWN

Ooey Gooey was a worm,
A mighty worm was he.
He stepped upon the railroad tracks,
The train he did not see!
Ooooey Gooooey!

2.
Celery

BY OGDEN NASH

Celery, raw,
Develops the jaw,
But celery, stewed,
Is more quietly chewed.

3.
The Little Man Who Wasn't There

BY HUGHES MEARNS

As I was going up the stair,
I met a man who wasn't there;
He wasn't there again today!
I wish, I *wish*, he'd stay away.

4.
The Vulture

BY HILAIRE BELLOC

The vulture eats between his meals,
And that's the reason why
He very, very rarely feels
As well as you or I.

His eye is dull. His head is bald,
His neck is growing thinner,
Oh, what a lesson for us all,
To only eat at dinner!

5.
After the Party

BY WILLIAM WISE

Jonathan Blake
Ate too much cake,
He isn't himself today;
He's tucked up in bed
With a feverish head,
And he doesn't much care to play.

Jonathan Blake
Ate too much cake,
And three kinds of ice cream too—
From his latest reports
He's quite out of sorts,
And I'm sure the reports are true.

I'm sorry to state
That he also ate
Six pickles, a pie, and a pear;
In fact I confess
It's a reasonable guess
He ate practically everything there.

Yes, Jonathan Blake
Ate too much cake,
So he's not at his best today;
But there's no need for sorrow—
If you come back tomorrow,
I'm sure he'll be out to play.

6.
Singing Time

BY ROSE FYLEMAN

I wake in the morning early
And always, the very first thing,
I poke out my head and I sit up in bed
And I sing and I sing and I sing.

7.
The Yak

BY HILAIRE BELLOC

As a friend to the children, commend me the Yak;
You will find it exactly the thing;
It will carry and fetch, you can ride on its back,
Or lead it about with a string.

The Tartar who dwells on the plains of Tibet
(A desolate region of snow),
Has for centuries made it a nursery pet,
And surely the Tartar should know!

Then tell your papa where the Yak can be got,
And if he is awfully rich,
He will buy you the creature—or else he will not
(I cannot be positive which).

8.
The Ingenious Little Old Man

BY JOHN BENNETT

A little old man of the sea
Went out in a boat for a sail:
The water came in
Almost up to his chin
And he had nothing with which to bail.

But this little old man of the sea
Just drew out his jack-knife so stout,
And a hole with its blade
In the bottom he made,
So that all of the water ran out.

9.
My Shadow

BY ROBERT LOUIS STEVENSON

I have a little shadow that goes in and out with me,
And what can be the use of him is more than I can see.
He is very, very like me from the heels up to the head;
And I see him jump before me, when I jump into my bed.

The funniest thing about him is the way he likes to grow—
Not at all like proper children, which is always very slow;
For he sometimes shoots up taller like an India-rubber ball,
And he sometimes gets so little that there's none of him at all.

He hasn't got a notion of how children ought to play,
And can only make a fool of me in every sort of way.
He stays so close beside me, he's a coward you can see;
I'd think shame to stick to nursie as that shadow sticks to me!

One morning, very early, before the sun was up,
I rose and found the shining dew on every buttercup;
But my lazy little shadow, like an arrant sleepyhead,
Had stayed at home behind me and was fast asleep in bed.

10.
There Was an Old Person Whose Habits

BY EDWARD LEAR

There was an Old Person whose habits
Induced him to feed upon rabbits;
When he'd eaten eighteen,
He turned perfectly green
Upon which he relinquished those habits.

11.
Jonathan Bing

BY BEATRICE CURTIS BROWN

Poor old Jonathan Bing
Went out in his carriage to visit the King,
But everyone pointed and said, "Look at that!
Jonathan Bing has forgotten his hat!"
(He'd forgotten his hat!)

Poor old Jonathan Bing
Went home and put on a new hat for the King,
But up by the palace a soldier said, "Hi!
You can't see the King; you've forgotten your tie!"
(He'd forgotten his tie!)

Poor old Jonathan Bing
He put on a *beautiful* tie for the King,
But when he arrived an Archbishop said, "Ho!
You can't come to court in pyjamas, you know!"

Poor old Jonathan Bing
Went home and addressed a short note to the King:
  If you please will excuse me
  I won't come to tea;
  For home's the best place for
  All people like me!

12.
Whole Duty of Children

BY ROBERT LOUIS STEVENSON

A child should always say what's true
And speak when he is spoken to,
And behave mannerly at table;
At least as far as he is able.

13.
Godfrey Gordon Gustavus Gore

BY WILLIAM BRIGHTY RANDS

Godfrey Gordon Gustavus Gore—
No doubt you have heard the name before—
Was a boy who never would shut a door!

The wind might whistle, the wind might roar,
And teeth be aching and throats be sore,
But still he never would shut the door.

His father would beg, his mother implore,
"Godfrey Gordon Gustavus Gore,
We really do wish you would shut the door!"

Their hands they wrung, their hair they tore;
But Godfrey Gordon Gustavus Gore
Was deaf as the buoy out at the Nore.

When he walked forth the folks would roar,
"Godfrey Gordon Gustavus Gore,
Why don't you think to shut the door?"

They rigged out a Shutter with sail and oar,
And threatened to pack off Gustavus Gore
On a voyage of penance to Singapore,

But he begged for mercy, and said, "No more!
Pray do not send me to Singapore
On a Shutter, and then I will shut the door!"

"You will?" said his parents; "then keep on shore!
But mind you do! For the plague is sore
Of a fellow that never will shut the door,
Godfrey Gordon Gustavus Gore!"

14.
My Gift

BY CHRISTINA ROSSETTI

What can I give Him
Poor as I am;
If I were a shepherd,
I would give Him a lamb.

If I were a wise man,
I would do my part.
Yet what I can I give Him,
Give my heart.

15.
The Swing

BY ROBERT LOUIS STEVENSON

How do you like to go up in a swing,
  Up in the air so blue?
Oh, I do think it the pleasantest thing
  Ever a child can do!

Up in the air and over the wall,
  'Till I can see so wide,
Rivers and trees and cattle and all
  Over the countryside—

'Till I look down on the garden green,
  Down on the roof so brown—
Up in the air I go flying again,
  Up in the air and down!

16.
Persevere

AUTHOR UNKNOWN

The fisher who draws in his net too soon,
Won't have any fish to sell;
The child who shuts up his book too soon,
Won't learn any lessons well.

If you would have your learning stay,
Be patient—don't learn too fast;
The man who travels a mile each day,
May get 'round the world at last.

17.
Who Has Seen the Wind?

BY CHRISTINA ROSSETTI

Who has seen the wind?
  Neither I nor you:
But when the leaves hang trembling
  The wind is passing through.

Who has seen the wind?
  Neither you nor I:
But when the trees bow down their heads
  The wind is passing by.

18.
The Eagle

BY ALFRED, LORD TENNYSON

He clasps the crag with crooked hands;
Close to the sun in lonely lands.
Ringed with the azure world, he stands.

The wrinkled sea beneath him crawls;
He watches from his mountain walls.
And like a thunderbolt he falls.

19.
The Swan and the Goose

BY WILLIAM ELLERY LEONARD

A rich man bought a Swan and Goose—
That for song, and this for use.
It chanced his simple-minded cook
One night the Swan for Goose mistook.

But in the dark about to chop
The Swan in two above the crop,
He heard the lyric note, and stayed
The action of the fatal blade.
  And thus we see a proper tune
  Is sometimes very opportune.

20.
Personal selection

Copy or attach your personal selection choice onto this page.

CERTIFICATE OF COMPLETION

This certifies that

____

has successfully completed the memorization
and presentation requirements for

LEVEL ONE OF
Linguistic Development through Poetry Memorization

____________________ ____________________

DATE SUPERVISOR

Listen. Speak. Read. Write. Think!

Level Two

Poems

Getting Started with Level Two

1. Begin working on the Level Two poems:
   a. Highlight the new poem.
   b. As you learn more poems, practice all the poems learned to date.
   c. Use the audio recording to help you.
2. Maintain the Level One poems using the lists on the right to guide you.

Level Two Poems

1 **How Doth the Little Crocodile** by Lewis Carroll
2 **At the Seaside** by Robert Louis Stevenson
3 **Rebecca, Who Slammed Doors for Fun and Perished Miserably** by Hilaire Belloc
4 **Fog** by Carl Sandburg
5 **Some One** by Walter de la Mare
6 **The Duke of Plaza-Toro** by W. S. Gilbert
7 **God and the Soldier** author unknown
8 **Jabberwocky** by Lewis Carroll
9 **The Height of the Ridiculous** by Oliver Wendell Holmes
10 **The Spider and the Fly** by Mary Howitt
11 **Trees** by Joyce Kilmer
12 **Ballad of the Tempest** by James T. Fields
13 **The Charge of the Light Brigade** by Alfred, Lord Tennyson
14 **Sea Fever** by John Masefield
15 **Shoes** by Louis Untermeyer
16 **The Glove and the Lions** by James Leigh Hunt
17 **Conscience and Remorse** by Paul Laurence Dunbar
18 **Stopping by Woods on a Snowy Evening** by Robert Frost
19 **Project** by Mary Fabyan Windeatt
20 **Personal selection** (8 lines or shorter): ______________

____

Level One Review

ODD NUMBERED DAYS

1 **Ooey Gooey**
3 **The Little Man Who Wasn't There**
5 **After the Party**
7 **The Yak**
9 **My Shadow**
11 **Jonathan Bing**
13 **Godfrey Gordon Gustavus Gore**
15 **The Swing**
17 **Who Has Seen the Wind?**
19 **The Swan and the Goose**

EVEN NUMBERED DAYS

2 **Celery**
4 **The Vulture**
6 **Singing Time**
8 **The Ingenious Little Old Man**
10 **There Was an Old Person Whose Habits**
12 **Whole Duty of Children**
14 **My Gift**
16 **Persevere**
18 **The Eagle**
20 **Personal selection:**

____

Below, check off the day when you have completed your poetry practice.

	1	2	3	4	5	6	7	8	9	10	11	12	13	14	15	16	17	18	19	20	21	22	23	24	25	26	27	28	29	30	31
Aug																															
Sep																															
Oct																															
Nov																															
Dec																															
Jan																															
Feb																															
Mar																															
Apr																															
May																															
Jun																															
Jul																															

1.
How Doth the Little Crocodile

BY LEWIS CARROLL

How doth the little crocodile
  Improve his shining tail,
And pour the waters of the Nile
  On every golden scale!

How cheerfully he seems to grin,
  How neatly spreads his claws,
And welcomes little fishes in
  With gently smiling jaws!

2.
At the Seaside

BY ROBERT LOUIS STEVENSON

When I was down beside the sea
A wooden spade they gave to me
  To dig the sandy shore.
My holes were empty like a cup.
In every hole the sea came up,
  'Till it could come no more.

3.
Rebecca, Who Slammed Doors for Fun and Perished Miserably

BY HILAIRE BELLOC

A trick that everyone abhors
In Little Girls is slamming Doors.
A Wealthy Banker's Little Daughter
Who lived in Palace Green, Bayswater
(By name Rebecca Offendort),
Was given to this Furious Sport.

She would deliberately go
And Slam the door like Billy-Ho!
To make her Uncle Jacob start.
She was not actually bad at heart,
But only rather rude and wild:
She was an aggravating child …

It happened that a Marble Bust
Of Abraham was standing just
Above the Door this little Lamb
Had carefully prepared to Slam,
And Down it came! It knocked her flat!
It laid her out! She looked like that.

Her Funeral Sermon (which was long
And followed by a Sacred Song)
Mentioned her Virtues, it is true,
But dwelt upon her Vices too,
And showed the Dreadful End of One
Who goes and slams the Door for Fun.

The children who were brought to hear
The awful Tale from far and near
Were much impressed, and inly swore
They never more would slam the Door.
—As often they had done before.

4.
Fog

BY CARL SANDBURG

The fog comes
on little cat feet.

It sits looking
over harbor and city
on silent haunches
and then, moves on.

5.
Some One

BY WALTER DE LA MARE

Some one came knocking
  At my wee, small door;
Some one came knocking,
  I'm sure—sure—sure;
I listened, I opened,
  I looked to left and right,
But nought there was a-stirring
  In the still dark night.
Only the busy beetle
  Tap-tapping in the wall,
Only from the forest
  The screech-owl's call,
Only the cricket whistling
  While the dewdrops fall,
So I know not who came knocking,
  At all, at all, at all.

6.
The Duke of Plaza-Toro

BY W.S. GILBERT

In enterprise of martial kind,
When there was any fighting,
He led his regiment from behind—
He found it less exciting.

But when away his regiment ran,
His place was at the fore, O—
That celebrated,
Cultivated,
Underrated
Nobleman,
The Duke of Plaza-Toro!

In the first and foremost flight, ha, ha!
You always found that knight, ha, ha!
That celebrated,
Cultivated,
Underrated
Nobleman,
The Duke of Plaza-Toro!

When, to evade Destruction's hand,
To hide they all proceeded,
No soldier in that gallant band
Hid half as well as he did.

He lay concealed throughout the war,
And so preserved his gore, O!
That unaffected,
Undetected,
Well-connected
Warrior,
The Duke of Plaza-Toro!

In every doughty deed, ha, ha!
He always took the lead, ha, ha!
That unaffected,
Undetected,
Well-connected
Warrior,
The Duke of Plaza-Toro!

7.
God and the Soldier

AUTHOR UNKNOWN

God and the Soldier
All men adore
In time of trouble,
And no more;
For when war is over
And all things righted
God is neglected—
The old soldier slighted.

8.
Jabberwocky

BY LEWIS CARROLL

'Twas brillig, and the slithy toves
  Did gyre and gimble in the wabe:
All mimsy were the borogoves,
  And the mome raths outgrabe.

"Beware the Jabberwock, my son!
  The jaws that bite, the claws that catch!
Beware the Jubjub bird, and shun
  The frumious Bandersnatch!"

He took his vorpal sword in hand:
  Long time the manxome foe he sought—
So rested he by the Tumtum tree,
  And stood awhile in thought.

And, as in uffish thought he stood,
  The Jabberwock, with eyes of flame,
Came whiffling through the tulgey wood,
  And burbled as it came!

One, two! One, two! And through and through
  The vorpal blade went snicker-snack!
He left it dead, and with its head
  He went galumphing back.

"And hast thou slain the Jabberwock?
  Come to my arms, my beamish boy!
O frabjous day! Callooh! Callay!"
  He chortled in his joy.

'Twas brillig, and the slithy toves
  Did gyre and gimble in the wabe:
All mimsy were the borogoves,
  And the mome raths outgrabe.

9.
The Height of the Ridiculous

BY OLIVER WENDELL HOLMES

I wrote some lines once on a time
In wondrous merry mood,
And thought, as usual, men would say
They were exceeding good.

They were so queer, so very queer,
I laughed as I would die;
Albeit, in the general way,
A sober man am I.

I called my servant, and he came;
How kind it was of him
To mind a slender man like me,
He of the mighty limb.

"These to the printer," I exclaimed,
And, in my humorous way,
I added (as a trifling jest),
"There'll be the devil to pay."

He took the paper, and I watched,
And saw him peep within;
At the first line he read, his face
Was all upon the grin.

He read the next; the grin grew broad,
And shot from ear to ear;
He read the third; a chuckling noise
I now began to hear.

The fourth: he broke into a roar;
The fifth: his waistband split;
The sixth: he burst five buttons off,
And tumbled in a fit.

Ten days and nights, with sleepless eye,
I watched that wretched man,
And since, I never dare to write
As funny as I can.

10.
The Spider and the Fly

BY MARY HOWITT

"Will you walk into my parlor?" said the Spider to the Fly,
" 'Tis the prettiest little parlor that ever you did spy;
The way into my parlor is up a winding stair,
And I have many curious things to show when you are there."
"Oh no, no," said the little Fly, "to ask me is in vain;
For who goes up your winding stair can ne'er come down again."

"I'm sure you must be weary, dear, with soaring up so high;
Will you rest upon my little bed?" said the Spider to the Fly.
"There are pretty curtains drawn around, the sheets are fine and thin;
And if you like to rest awhile, I'll snugly tuck you in!"
"Oh no, no," said the little Fly, "for I've often heard it said
They never, never wake again, who sleep upon your bed!"

Said the cunning Spider to the Fly, "Dear friend, what can I do
To prove the warm affection I've always felt for you?
I have within my pantry, good store of all that's nice;
I'm sure you're very welcome—will you please to take a slice?"
"Oh no, no," said the little Fly, "kind sir, that cannot be,
I've heard what's in your pantry, and I do not wish to see!"

"Sweet creature," said the Spider, "you're witty and you're wise;
How handsome are your gauzy wings, how brilliant are your eyes!
I have a little looking-glass upon my parlor shelf;
If you'll step in one moment, dear, you shall behold yourself."
"I thank you, gentle sir," she said, "for what you're pleased to say,
And bidding you good-morning now, I'll call another day."

The spider turned him round about, and went into his den,
For well he knew the silly Fly would soon come back again;
So he wove a subtle web in a little corner sly,
And set his table ready to dine upon the Fly.

CONTINUED ON NEXT PAGE ›

Then he came out to his door again, and merrily did sing,
"Come hither, hither, pretty Fly, with the pearl and silver wing;
Your robes are green and purple, there's a crest upon your head;
Your eyes are like the diamond bright, but mine are dull as lead."

Alas, alas, how very soon this silly little Fly,
Hearing his wily, flattering words, came slowly flitting by;
With buzzing wings she hung aloft, then near and nearer drew—
Thinking only of her brilliant eyes, and green and purple hue;
Thinking only of her crested head—poor foolish thing! At last,
Up jumped the cunning Spider, and fiercely held her fast.
He dragged her up his winding stair, into his dismal den
Within his little parlor—but she ne'er came out again!

And now, dear little children, who may this story read,
To idle, silly, flattering words, I pray you ne'er give heed;
Unto an evil counselor close heart, and ear, and eye,
And take a lesson from this tale of the Spider and the Fly.

11.
Trees

BY JOYCE KILMER

I think that I shall never see
A poem lovely as a tree.

A tree whose hungry mouth is prest
Against the earth's sweet flowing breast;

A tree that looks at God all day,
And lifts her leafy arms to pray;

A tree that may in Summer wear
A nest of robins in her hair;

Upon whose bosom snow has lain;
Who intimately lives with rain.

Poems are made by fools like me,
But only God can make a tree.

12.
Ballad of the Tempest

BY JAMES T. FIELDS

We were crowded in the cabin,
  Not a soul would dare to sleep—
It was midnight on the waters,
  And a storm was on the deep.

'Tis a fearful thing in winter
  To be shattered by the blast,
And to hear the rattling trumpet
  Thunder, "Cut away the mast!"

So we shuddered there in silence—
  For the stoutest held his breath,
While the hungry sea was roaring
  And the breakers talked with Death.

As thus we sat in darkness,
  Each one busy with his prayers,
"We are lost!" the captain shouted
  As he staggered down the stairs.

But his little daughter whispered,
  As she took his icy hand,
"Isn't God upon the ocean,
  Just the same as on the land?"

Then we kissed the little maiden,
  And we spoke in better cheer,
And we anchored safe in harbor
  When the morn was shining clear.

13.
The Charge of the Light Brigade

BY ALFRED, LORD TENNYSON

Half a league, half a league,
Half a league onward,
All in the valley of Death
  Rode the six hundred.

"Forward the Light Brigade!
Charge for the guns!" he said.
Into the valley of Death
  Rode the six hundred.

"Forward, the Light Brigade!"
Was there a man dismayed?
Not though the soldier knew
  Some one had blundered.

Theirs not to make reply,
Theirs not to reason why,
Theirs but to do and die.
Into the valley of Death
  Rode the six hundred.

Cannon to right of them,
Cannon to left of them,
Cannon in front of them
  Volleyed and thundered;
Stormed at with shot and shell,
Boldly they rode and well,
Into the jaws of Death,
Into the mouth of Hell
  Rode the six hundred.

Flashed all their sabers bare,
Flashed as they turned in air
Sabring the gunners there,
Charging an army, while
  All the world wondered.

Plunged in the battery-smoke
Right through the line they broke;
Cossack and Russian
Reeled from the sabre-stroke
Shattered and sundered.
Then they rode back, but not,
  Not the six hundred.

Cannon to right of them,
Cannon to left of them,
Cannon behind them
  Volleyed and thundered;
Stormed at with shot and shell,
While horse and hero fell,
They that had fought so well
Came through the jaws of Death,
Back from the mouth of Hell,
All that was left of them,
  Left of six hundred.

When can their glory fade?
Oh, the wild charge they made!
  All the world wondered.
Honor the charge they made!
Honor the Light Brigade,
  Noble six hundred!

14.
Sea Fever

BY JOHN MASEFIELD

I must go down to the seas again, to the lonely sea and the sky,
And all I ask is a tall ship and a star to steer her by,
And the wheel's kick and the wind's song and the white sail's shaking,
And a gray mist on the sea's face, and a gray dawn breaking.

I must go down to the seas again, for the call of the running tide
Is a wild call and a clear call that may not be denied;
And all I ask is a windy day with the white clouds flying,
And the flung spray and the blown spume, and the sea gulls crying.

I must go down to the seas again, to the vagrant gypsy life,
To the gull's way and the whale's way where the wind's like a whetted knife;
And all I ask is a merry yarn from a laughing fellow-rover,
And quiet sleep and a sweet dream when the long trick's over.

15.
Shoes

BY LOUIS UNTERMEYER

I think that no one ever knew
A poem lovely as a shoe.

A shoe that has so much of grace,
Tied and adorned with its own lace.

A shoe that will, in winter, wear
Rubbers to skid with everywhere.

A shoe that points to its own goal,
And looks well-heeled to save its sole.

Poems are made by fools like you.
But one old woman lived in a shoe!

16.
The Glove and the Lions

BY JAMES LEIGH HUNT

King Francis was a hearty king, and loved a royal sport,
And one day, as his lions fought, sat looking on the court;
The nobles filled the benches round, the ladies by their side,
And 'mongst them sat the Count de Lorge, with one for whom he sighed:
And truly 't was a gallant thing to see that crowning show,
Valor and love, and a king above, and the royal beasts below.

Ramped and roared the lions, with horrid laughing jaws;
They bit, they glared, gave blows like beams, a wind went with their paws;
With wallowing might and stifled roar, they rolled on one another:
'Till all the pit, with sand and mane, was in a thunderous smother;
The bloody foam above the bars came whizzing through the air:
Said Francis, then, "Faith, gentlemen, we're better here than there."

De Lorge's love o'erheard the king,–a beauteous, lively dame,
With smiling lips, and sharp, bright eyes, which always seemed the same;
She thought, "The Count, my lover, is brave as brave can be,
He surely would do wondrous things to show his love for me;
King, ladies, lovers, all look on; the occasion is divine;
I'll drop my glove to prove his love; great glory will be mine."

She dropped her glove to prove his love, then looked at him and smiled;
He bowed, and in a moment leaped among the lions wild;
The leap was quick, return was quick, he soon regained his place,
Then threw the glove, but not with love, right in the lady's face.
"In faith," cried Francis, "rightly done!" and he rose from where he sat;
"No love," quoth he, "but vanity, sets love a task like that."

17.
Conscience and Remorse

BY PAUL LAURENCE DUNBAR

"Good-bye," I said to my conscience–
"Good-bye for aye and aye,"
And I put her hands off harshly,
And turned my face away;
And conscience smitten sorely
Returned not from that day.

But a time came when my spirit
Grew weary of its pace;
And I cried: "Come back, my conscience;
I long to see thy face."
But conscience cried; "I cannot;
Remorse sits in my place."

18.
Stopping by Woods on a Snowy Evening

BY ROBERT FROST

Whose woods these are I think I know.
His house is in the village, though;
He will not see me stopping here
To watch his woods fill up with snow.

My little horse must think it queer
To stop without a farmhouse near
Between the woods and frozen lake
The darkest evening of the year.

He gives his harness bells a shake
To ask if there is some mistake.
The only other sound's the sweep
Of easy wind and downy flake.

The woods are lovely, dark, and deep,
But I have promises to keep,
and miles to go before I sleep.
And miles to go before I sleep.

19.
Project

BY MARY FABYAN WINDEATT

Now it is well
That we should start
Planning a Fortress
In the Heart;

Building with things
Which will endure
Longer than Sorrow's
Signature

(Take away stone,
Take away wood;
Faith is ten thousand
Times as good)

Take away steel,
Take away lead;
Charity, hope, will
Do instead!

Thus when the years
Pile up the pain
We can go seeking
Peace again;

Back of the walls
Heaven designed
Just for the hurts of
Humankind.

20.
Personal selection

Copy or attach your personal selection choice onto this page.

CERTIFICATE OF COMPLETION

This certifies that

____

has successfully completed the memorization
and presentation requirements for

LEVEL TWO OF
Linguistic Development through Poetry Memorization

DATE

Listen. Speak. Read. Write. Think!

SUPERVISOR

Level Three

Poems

Getting Started with Level Three

1. Use the list below to to keep track of the poems you are working on.
2. Use the lists on the next page to maintain poems from Levels One and Two.

Level Three Poems

1 **A Young Lady Named Bright** by Edward Lear
2 **A Psalm of Life** by Henry Wadsworth Longfellow
3 **The Road Not Taken** by Robert Frost
4 **O Captain! My Captain!** by Walt Whitman
5 **Matilda, Who Told Lies, and Was Burned to Death** by Hilaire Belloc
6 **Scintillate, Scintillate, Globule Vivific** by Dave Arns
7 **What I Live For** by George Linnaeus Banks
8 **Courage** by Sister M. Eulalia, RSM
9 **Grandfather's Clock** by Henry Clay Work
10 **The Touch of the Master's Hand** by Myra Brooks Welch
11 **The Unknown Soldier** by Billy Rose
12 **The Pessimist** by Ben King; **The Optimist** author unknown
13 **The Fool's Prayer** by Edward Roland Sill
14 **Casey at the Bat** by Ernest Lawrence Thayer
15 **He Wishes for the Cloths of Heaven** by W.B. Yeats
16 **The Destruction of Sennacherib** by Lord Byron
17 **The Village Blacksmith** by Henry Wadsworth Longfellow
18 **When I Heard the Learn'd Astronomer** by Walt Whitman
19 **Casey's Revenge** by Grantland Rice
20 **Personal selection** (8 lines or shorter): ____________

____

Maintaining Levels One and Two

The lists on the next page will help you maintain the poems from the other levels.

Below, check off the day when you have completed your poetry practice. The letters in the chart refer to the maintenance lists on the next page. The last day of each month is serendipity.* Choose your favorite poems from any list to recite for review.

	1	2	3	4	5	6	7	8	9	10	11	12	13	14	15	16	17	18	19	20	21	22	23	24	25	26	27	28	29	30	31
Aug	A	B	C	D	A	B	C	D	A	B	C	D	A	B	C	D	A	B	C	D	A	B	C	D	A	B	C	D	A	B	★
Sep	C	D	A	B	C	D	A	B	C	D	A	B	C	D	A	B	C	D	A	B	C	D	A	B	C	D	A	B	C	★	/
Oct	D	A	B	C	D	A	B	C	D	A	B	C	D	A	B	C	D	A	B	C	D	A	B	C	D	A	B	C	D	A	★
Nov	B	C	D	A	B	C	D	A	B	C	D	A	B	C	D	A	B	C	D	A	B	C	D	A	B	C	D	A	B	★	/
Dec	C	D	A	B	C	D	A	B	C	D	A	B	C	D	A	B	C	D	A	B	C	D	A	B	C	D	A	B	C	D	★
Jan	A	B	C	D	A	B	C	D	A	B	C	D	A	B	C	D	A	B	C	D	A	B	C	D	A	B	C	D	A	B	★
Feb	C	D	A	B	C	D	A	B	C	D	A	B	C	D	A	B	C	D	A	B	C	D	A	B	C	D	A	B	★	/	/
Mar	C	D	A	B	C	D	A	B	C	D	A	B	C	D	A	B	C	D	A	B	C	D	A	B	C	D	A	B	C	D	★
Apr	A	B	C	D	A	B	C	D	A	B	C	D	A	B	C	D	A	B	C	D	A	B	C	D	A	B	C	D	A	★	/
May	B	C	D	A	B	C	D	A	B	C	D	A	B	C	D	A	B	C	D	A	B	C	D	A	B	C	D	A	B	C	★
Jun	D	A	B	C	D	A	B	C	D	A	B	C	D	A	B	C	D	A	B	C	D	A	B	C	D	A	B	C	D	★	/
Jul	A	B	C	D	A	B	C	D	A	B	C	D	A	B	C	D	A	B	C	D	A	B	C	D	A	B	C	D	A	B	★

* Serendipity refers to a pleasant, unexpected surprise or discovery.

Maintaining Levels One and Two

Use these lists to maintain earlier levels while you are learning the first ten poems of Level Three.

List A

LEVEL ONE

1 Ooey Gooey
5 After the Party
9 My Shadow
13 Godfrey Gordon Gustavus Gore
17 Who Has Seen the Wind?

LEVEL TWO

1 How Doth the Little Crocodile
3 Rebecca, Who Slammed Doors for Fun
5 Some One
7 God and the Soldier
9 The Height of the Ridiculous
11 Trees
13 The Charge of the Light Brigade
15 Shoes
17 Conscience and Remorse
19 Project

List B

LEVEL ONE

2 Celery
6 Singing Time
10 There Was an Old Person Whose Habits
14 My Gift
18 The Eagle

LEVEL TWO

2 At the Seaside
4 Fog
6 The Duke of Plaza-Toro
8 Jabberwocky
10 The Spider and the Fly
12 Ballad of the Tempest
14 Sea Fever
16 The Glove and the Lions
18 Stopping by Woods on a Snowy Evening
20 Personal Selection: ____________

List C

LEVEL ONE

3 The Little Man Who Wasn't There
7 The Yak
11 Jonathan Bing
15 The Swing
19 The Swan and the Goose

LEVEL TWO

1 How Doth the Little Crocodile
3 Rebecca, Who Slammed Doors for Fun
5 Some One
7 God and the Soldier
9 The Height of the Ridiculous
11 Trees
13 The Charge of the Light Brigade
15 Shoes
17 Conscience and Remorse
19 Project

List D

LEVEL ONE

4 The Vulture
8 The Ingenious Little Old Man
12 Whole Duty of Children
16 Persevere
20 Personal Selection: ____________

LEVEL TWO

2 At the Seaside
4 Fog
6 The Duke of Plaza-Toro
8 Jabberwocky
10 The Spider and the Fly
12 Ballad of the Tempest
14 Sea Fever
16 The Glove and the Lions
18 Stopping by Woods on a Snowy Evening
20 Personal Selection: ____________

Use these lists to maintain earlier levels while you are learning the last ten poems of Level Three.

List A

LEVEL ONE

1 Ooey Gooey
5 After the Party
9 My Shadow
13 Godfrey Gordon Gustavus Gore
17 Who Has Seen the Wind?

LEVEL TWO

1 How Doth the Little Crocodile
5 Some One
9 The Height of the Ridiculous
13 The Charge of the Light Brigade
17 Conscience and Remorse

List B

LEVEL ONE

2 Celery
6 Singing Time
10 There Was an Old Person Whose Habits
14 My Gift
18 The Eagle

LEVEL TWO

2 At the Seaside
6 The Duke of Plaza-Toro
10 The Spider and the Fly
14 Sea Fever
18 Stopping by Woods on a Snowy Evening

List C

LEVEL ONE

3 The Little Man Who Wasn't There
7 The Yak
11 Jonathan Bing
15 The Swing
19 The Swan and the Goose

LEVEL TWO

3 Rebecca, Who Slammed Doors for Fun
7 God and the Soldier
11 Trees
15 Shoes
19 Project

List D

LEVEL ONE

4 The Vulture
8 The Ingenious Little Old Man
12 Whole Duty of Children
16 Persevere
20 Personal Selection: ____________

LEVEL TWO

4 Fog
8 Jabberwocky
12 Ballad of the Tempest
16 The Glove and the Lions
20 Personal Selection: ____________

1.
A Young Lady Named Bright

BY EDWARD LEAR

There was a young lady named Bright,
Who traveled much faster than light.
  She started one day
  In the relative way,
And returned on the previous night.

2.
A Psalm of Life

BY HENRY WADSWORTH LONGFELLOW

Tell me not, in mournful numbers,
Life is but an empty dream!—
For the soul is dead that slumbers,
And things are not what they seem.

Life is real! Life is earnest!
And the grave is not its goal;
Dust thou art, to dust returnest,
Was not spoken of the soul.

Not enjoyment, and not sorrows,
Is our destined end or way;
But to act, that each to-morrow
Find us farther than to-day.

Art is long, and Time is fleeting,
And our hearts, though stout and brave,
Still, like muffled drums, are beating
Funeral marches to the grave.

In the world's broad field of battle,
In the bivouac of Life,
Be not like dumb, driven cattle!
Be a hero in the strife!

Trust no future, howe'er pleasant!
Let the dead Past bury its dead!
Act, —act in the living Present!
Heart within, and God o'erhead!

Lives of great men all remind us
We can make our lives sublime,
And, departing, leave behind us
Footprints on the sands of time;

Footprints, that perhaps another,
Sailing o'er life's solemn main,
A forlorn and shipwrecked brother,
Seeing, shall take heart again.

Let us, then, be up and doing,
With a heart for any fate;
Still achieving, still pursuing,
Learn to labor and to wait.

3.
The Road Not Taken

BY ROBERT FROST

Two roads diverged in a yellow wood,
And sorry I could not travel both
And be one traveler, long I stood
And looked down one as far as I could
To where it bent in the undergrowth;

Then took the other, as just as fair,
And having perhaps the better claim,
Because it was grassy and wanted wear;
Though as for that the passing there
Had worn them really about the same,

And both that morning equally lay
In leaves no step had trodden black.
Oh, I kept the first for another day!
Yet knowing how way leads on to way,
I doubted if I should ever come back.

I shall be telling this with a sigh
Somewhere ages and ages hence;
Two roads diverged in a wood, and I—
I took the one less traveled by,
And that has made all the difference.

4.
O Captain! My Captain!

BY WALT WHITMAN

O Captain! My Captain! our fearful trip is done,
The ship has weathered every rack, the prize we sought is won,
The port is near, the bells I hear, the people all exulting,
While follow eyes the steady keel, the vessel grim and daring;

But O heart! heart! heart!
O the bleeding drops of red,
Where on the deck my Captain lies,
Fallen cold and dead.

O Captain! My Captain! rise up and hear the bells;
Rise up—for you the flag is flung—for you the bugle trills,
For you bouquets and ribboned wreaths—for you the shores a-crowding,
For you they call, the swaying mass, their eager faces turning;

Here Captain! dear father!
This arm beneath your head!
It is some dream that on the deck
You've fallen cold and dead.

My Captain does not answer, his lips are pale and still,
My father does not feel my arm, he has no pulse nor will,
The ship is anchored safe and sound, its voyage closed and done,
From fearful trip the victor ship comes in with object won;

Exult O shores, and ring O bells!
But I, with mournful tread,
Walk the deck my Captain lies,
Fallen cold and dead.

5.

Matilda, Who Told Lies, and Was Burned to Death

BY HILAIRE BELLOC

Matilda told such Dreadful Lies,
It made one Gasp and Stretch one's Eyes;
Her Aunt, who, from her Earliest Youth,
Had kept a Strict Regard for Truth,
Attempted to believe Matilda:
The effort very nearly killed her,
And would have done so, had not She
Discovered this Infirmity.

For once, towards the Close of Day,
Matilda, growing tired of play,
And finding she was left alone,
Went tiptoe to the Telephone
And summoned the Immediate Aid
Of London's Noble Fire-Brigade.

Within an hour the gallant Band
Were pouring in on every hand,
From Putney, Hackney Downs, and Bow
With Courage high and Hearts a-glow
They galloped, roaring through the Town,
"Matilda's House is Burning Down!"
Inspired by British Cheers and Loud
Proceeding from the Crowd,

They ran their ladders through a Score
Of windows on the Ball Room Floor;
And took Peculiar Pains to Souse
The Pictures up and down the House,
Until Matilda's Aunt succeeded
In showing them they were not needed;
And even then she had to Pay
To get the Men to go Away!

It happened that a few Weeks later
Her Aunt was off to the Theatre
To see that Interesting Play
The Second Mrs. Tanqueray.
She had refused to take her Niece
To hear this Entertaining Piece:
(A Deprivation Just and Wise
To punish her for Telling Lies.)

That night a Fire *did* break out—
You should have heard Matilda Shout!
You should have heard her Scream and Bawl,
And throw the window up and call
To People passing in the Street—
(The rapidly increasing Heat
Encouraging her to obtain
Their confidence)—but all In Vain!

For every time She shouted, "Fire!"
They only answered, "Little Liar!"
And therefore when her Aunt returned,
Matilda, and the House, were Burned.

6.
Scintillate, Scintillate, Globule Vivific

BY DAVE ARNS

Scintillate, scintillate, globule vivific!
In vain do I ponder thy nature specific—
  Precariously poised in the ether capacious,
  Closely resembling a gem carbonaceous;
Scintillate, scintillate, globule vivific,
In vain do I ponder thy nature specific!

7.
What I Live For

BY GEORGE LINNAEUS BANKS

I live for those who love me,
Whose hearts are kind and true;
For the heaven that smiles above me,
And awaits my spirit, too;
For all human ties that bind me,
For the task by God assigned me,
For the bright hopes left behind me,
And the good that I can do.

I live to learn their story,
Who've suffered for my sake;
To emulate their glory,
And follow in their wake;
Bards, patriots, martyrs, sages,
The noble of all ages,
Whose deeds crown History's pages,
And Time's great volume make.

I live to hold communion
With all that is divine;
To feel there is a union
'Twixt Nature's heart and mine;
To profit by affliction,
Reap truths from fields of fiction,
Grow wiser from conviction,
And fulfill each grand design.

I live to hail that season,
By gifted minds foretold,
When men shall live by reason,
And not alone by gold;
When man to man united,
And every wrong thing righted,
The whole world shall be lighted
As Eden was of old.

I live for those who love me,
For those who know me true;
For the heaven that smiles above me,
And awaits my spirit too;
For the cause that lacks assistance,
For the wrong that needs resistance,
For the future in the distance,
And the good that I can do.

8.
Courage

BY SISTER M. EULALIA, RSM

Courage is a fabric
  So woven of the soul
It shrinks with fear, stretches
  When straining toward a Goal.
But when in eyes it glows
  Awaiting tyrant's rod,
It is of mystic birth,
  Holding a tryst with God.

9.
Grandfather's Clock

BY HENRY CLAY WORK

My grandfather's clock
  was too large for the shelf,
So it stood ninety years on the floor;
It was taller by half
  than the old man himself,
Though it weighed not a pennyweight more.
It was bought on the morn
  of the day that he was born
And was always his treasure and pride,
But it stopped short—never to go again—
When the old man died.

Ninety years without slumbering—
Tick, tick, tick, tick.
His life seconds numbering—
Tick, tick, tick, tick.
It stopped short—never to go again—
When the old man died.

In watching its pendulum swing to and fro
Many hours had he spent while a boy;
And in childhood and manhood
  the clock seemed to know
And to share both his grief and his joy,
For it struck twenty-four
  when he entered the door
With a blooming and beautiful bride,
But it stopped short—never to go again—
When the old man died.

My grandfather said of those he could hire,
Not a servant so faithful he found,
For it wasted no time and had but one desire—
At the close of each week to be wound.
And it kept in its place—
  not a frown upon its face,
And its hands never hung by its side;
But it stopped short—never to go again—
When the old man died.

It rang an alarm in the dead of night—
An alarm that for years had been dumb.
And we knew that his spirit
  was pluming for flight,
That his hour for departure had come.
Still the clock kept the time
  with a soft and muffled chime
As we silently stood by his side;
But it stopped short—never to go again—
When the old man died.

10.
The Touch of the Master's Hand

BY MYRA BROOKS WELCH

'Twas battered and scarred, and the auctioneer
Thought it scarcely worth his while
To waste much time on the old violin,
But held it up with a smile:
"What am I bidden, good folks," he cried,
"Who'll start the bidding for me?"
"A dollar, a dollar"; then "Two! Only two?
Two dollars, and who'll make it three?
Three dollars, once; three dollars, twice;
Going for three"—But no,
From the room, far back, a gray-haired man
Came forward and picked up the bow;
Then, wiping the dust from the old violin,
And tightening the loose strings,
He played a melody pure and sweet
As a caroling angel sings.

The music ceased, and the auctioneer,
With a voice that was quiet and low,
Said: "What am I bid for the old violin?"
And he held it up with the bow.
"A thousand dollars, and who'll make it two?
Two thousand! And who'll make it three?
Three thousand, once, three thousand, twice,
And going, and gone," said he.
The people cheered, but some of them cried,
"We do not quite understand
What changed its worth." Swift came the reply:
"The touch of a master's hand."

And many a man with life out of tune,
And battered and scarred with sin,
Is auctioned cheap to the thoughtless crowd,
Much like the old violin.
A "mess of pottage," a glass of wine;
A game—and he travels on.
He is "going" once, and "going" twice,
He's "going" and almost "gone."
But the Master comes, and the foolish crowd
Never can quite understand
The worth of a soul and the change that's wrought
By the touch of the Master's hand.

11.
The Unknown Soldier

BY BILLY ROSE

There's a graveyard near the White House
 Where the Unknown Soldier lies,
And the flowers there are sprinkled
 With the tears from mother's eyes.

I stood there not so long ago
 With roses for the brave,
And suddenly I heard a voice
 Speak from out the grave:

"I am the Unknown Soldier,"
 The spirit voice began,
"And I think I have the right
 To ask some questions man to man.

Are my buddies taken care of?
 Was their victory so sweet?
Is that big reward you offered
 Selling pencils on the street?

Did they really win the freedom
 They battled to achieve?
Do you still respect that *Croix de Guerre*
 Above that empty sleeve?

Does a gold star in the window
 Now mean anything at all?
I wonder how my old girl feels
 When she hears a bugle call.

And that baby who sang
 'Hello, Central, give me no man's land'–
Can they replace her daddy
 With a military band?

I wonder if the profiteers
 Have satisfied their greed?
I wonder if a soldier's mother
 Ever is in need?

I wonder if the kings, who planned it all
 Are really satisfied?
They played their game of checkers
 And eleven million died.

I am the Unknown Soldier
 And maybe I died in vain,
But if I were alive and my country called,
 I'd do it all over again."

12.

The Pessimist

BY BEN KING

Nothing to do but work,
Nothing to eat but food;
Nothing to wear but clothes
To keep one from going nude.

Nothing to breathe but air,
Quick as a flash 'tis gone;
Nowhere to fall but off,
Nowhere to stand but on.

Nothing to comb but hair,
Nowhere to sleep but in bed;
Nothing to weep but tears,
Nothing to bury but dead.

Nothing to sing but songs;
Ah, well, alas! alack!
Nowhere to go but out,
Nowhere to come but back.

Nothing to see but sights,
Nothing to quench but thirst;
Nothing to have but what we've got;
Thus thro' life we are cursed.

Nothing to strike but a gait;
Everything moves that goes.
Nothing at all but common sense
Can ever withstand these woes.

The Optimist

AUTHOR UNKNOWN

The optimist fell ten stories,
At each window bar
He shouted to his friends,
"All right so far."

13.
The Fool's Prayer

BY EDWARD ROWLAND SILL

The royal feast was done; the King
Sought some new sport to banish care,
And to his jester cried: "Sir Fool,
Kneel now, and make for us a prayer!"

The jester doffed his cap and bells,
And stood the mocking court before;
They could not see the bitter smile
Behind the painted grin he wore.

He bowed his head, and bent his knee
Upon the Monarch's silken stool;
His pleading voice arose: "O Lord,
Be merciful to me, a fool!

"No pity, Lord, could change the heart
From red with wrong to white as wool;
The rod must heal the sin: but Lord,
Be merciful to me, a fool!

"'Tis not by guilt the onward sweep
Of truth and right, O Lord, we stay;
'Tis by our follies that so long
We hold the earth from heaven away.

"These clumsy feet, still in the mire,
Go crushing blossoms without end;
These hard, well-meaning hands we thrust
Among the heart-strings of a friend.

"The ill-timed truth we might have kept—
Who knows how sharp it pierced and stung?
The word we had not sense to say—
Who knows how grandly it had rung!

"Our faults no tenderness should ask.
The chastening stripes must cleanse them all;
But for our blunders—oh, in shame
Before the eyes of heaven we fall.

"Earth bears no balsam for mistakes;
Men crown the knave, and scourge the tool
That did his will; but Thou, O Lord,
Be merciful to me, a fool!"

The room was hushed; in silence rose
The King, and sought his gardens cool,
And walked apart, and murmured low,
"Be merciful to me, a fool!"

14.
Casey at the Bat

BY ERNEST LAWRENCE THAYER

The outlook wasn't brilliant for the Mudville nine that day;
The score stood four to two but one inning more to play.
And then when Cooney died at first and Barrows did the same,
A sickly silence fell upon the patrons of the game.

A straggling few got up to go in deep despair. The rest
Clung to the hope which springs eternal in the human breast;
They thought if only Casey could but get a whack at that—
We'd put up even money now with Casey at the bat.

But Flynn preceded Casey, as did also Jimmy Blake,
And the former was a lulu and the latter was a cake;
So upon that stricken multitude grim melancholy sat,
For there seemed but little chance of Casey's getting to the bat.

But Flynn let drive a single, to the wonderment of all,
And Blake, the much despised, tore the cover off the ball;
And when the dust had lifted, and the men saw what had occurred,
There was Jimmy safe at second and Flynn a-hugging third.

Then from five thousand throats and more there rose a lusty yell;
It rumbled through the valley, it rattled in the dell;
It knocked upon the mountain and recoiled upon the flat,
For Casey, mighty Casey, was advancing to the bat.

There was ease in Casey's manner as he stepped into his place;
There was pride in Casey's bearing and a smile on Casey's face.
And when, responding to the cheers, he lightly doffed his hat,
No stranger in the crowd could doubt 'twas Casey at the bat.

Ten thousand eyes were on him as he rubbed his hands with dirt;
Five thousand tongues applauded when he wiped them on his shirt.
Then while the writhing pitcher ground the ball into his hip,
Defiance gleamed in Casey's eye, a sneer curled Casey's lip.

CONTINUED ON NEXT PAGE >

And now the leather-covered sphere came hurtling through the air,
And Casey stood a-watching it in haughty grandeur there.
Close by the sturdy batsman the ball unheeded sped—
"That ain't my style," said Casey. "Strike one," the umpire said.

From the benches, black with people, there went up a muffled roar,
Like the beating of the storm waves on a stern and distant shore.
"Kill him! Kill the umpire!" shouted someone on the stand;
And it's likely they'd have killed him had not Casey raised his hand.

With a smile of Christian charity great Casey's visage shone;
He stilled the rising tumult; he bade the game go on;
He signaled to the pitcher, and once more the spheroid flew;
But Casey still ignored it, and the umpire said, "Strike two."

"Fraud!" cried the maddened thousands, and echo answered, "Fraud!"
But one scornful look from Casey and the audience was awed.
They saw his face grow stern and cold, they saw his muscles strain,
And they knew that Casey wouldn't let that ball go by again.

The sneer is gone from Casey's lip, his teeth are clenched in hate;
He pounds with cruel violence his bat upon the plate.
And now the pitcher holds the ball, and now he lets it go,
And now the air is shattered by the force of Casey's blow.

Oh, somewhere in this favored land the sun is shining bright;
The band is playing somewhere, and somewhere hearts are light,
And somewhere men are laughing, and somewhere children shout;
But there is no joy in Mudville—mighty Casey has struck out.

15.
He Wishes for the Cloths of Heaven

BY W.B. YEATS

Had I the heavens' embroidered cloths,
Enwrought with golden and silver light,
The blue and the dim and the dark cloths
Of night and light and the half-light,
I would spread the cloths under your feet;
But I, being poor, have only my dreams;
I have spread my dreams under your feet;
Tread softly because you tread on my dreams.

16.
The Destruction of Sennacherib

BY LORD BYRON

The Assyrian came down like the wolf on the fold,
And his cohorts were gleaming in purple and gold;
And the sheen of their spears was like stars on the sea,
When the blue wave rolls nightly on deep Galilee.

Like the leaves of the forest when Summer is green,
That host with their banners at sunset were seen:
Like the leaves of the forest when Autumn hath flown,
That host on the morrow lay withered and strown.

For the Angel of Death spread his wings on the blast,
And breathed in the face of the foe as he passed;
And the eyes of the sleepers waxed deadly and chill,
And their hearts but once heaved, and forever grew still.

And there lay the steed with his nostril all wide,
But through it there rolled not the breath of his pride;
And the foam of his gasping lay white on the turf,
And cold as the spray of the rock-beating surf.

And there lay the rider distorted and pale,
With the dew on his brow, and the rust on his mail;
And the tents were all silent, the banners alone,
The lances unlifted, the trumpet unblown.

And the widows of Ashur are loud in their wail,
And the idols are broke in the temple of Baal;
And the might of the Gentile, unsmote by the sword,
Hath melted like snow in the glance of the Lord!

17. The Village Blacksmith

BY HENRY WADSWORTH LONGFELLOW

Under a spreading chestnut-tree
The village smithy stands;
The smith, a mighty man is he,
With large and sinewy hands;
And the muscles of his brawny arms
Are strong as iron bands.

His hair is crisp, and black, and long,
His face is like the tan;
His brow is wet with honest sweat,
He earns whate'er he can,
And looks the whole world
in the face,
For he owes not any man.

Week in, week out,
from morn till night,
You can hear his bellows blow;
You can hear him
swing his heavy sledge,
With measured beat and slow,
Like a sexton ringing the village bell,
When the evening sun is low.

And children coming
home from school
Look in at the open door;
They love to see the flaming forge,
And hear the bellows roar,
And catch the burning sparks that fly
Like chaff from a threshing-floor.

He goes on Sunday to the church,
And sits among his boys;
He hears the parson pray and preach,
He hears his daughter's voice,
Singing in the village choir,
And it makes his heart rejoice.

It sounds to him like her mother's voice,
Singing in Paradise!
He needs must think of her once more,
How in the grave she lies;
And with his hard, rough hand he wipes
A tear out of his eyes.

Toiling,—rejoicing,—sorrowing,
Onward through life he goes;
Each morning sees some task begin,
Each evening sees it close;
Something attempted, something done,
Has earned a night's repose.

Thanks, thanks to thee, my worthy friend,
For the lesson thou hast taught!
Thus at the flaming forge of life
Our fortunes must be wrought;
Thus on its sounding anvil shaped
Each burning deed and thought!

18.
When I Heard the Learn'd Astronomer

BY WALT WHITMAN

When I heard the learn'd astronomer;
When the proofs, the figures, were ranged in columns before me;
When I was shown the charts and the diagrams,
  to add, divide, and measure them;
When I, sitting, heard the astronomer,
  where he lectured with much applause in the lecture-room,
How soon, unaccountable, I became tired and sick;
Till rising and gliding out, I wander'd off by myself,
In the mystical moist night-air, and from time to time,
Look'd up in perfect silence at the stars.

19.
Casey's Revenge

BY GRANTLAND RICE

There were saddened hearts in Mudville for a week or even more;
There were muttered oaths and curses—every fan in town was sore.
"Just think," said one, "how soft it looked with Casey at the bat!
And then to think he'd go and spring a bush-league trick like that."

All his past fame was forgotten; he was now a hopeless "shine,"
They called him "Strike-out Casey" from the mayor down the line,
And as he came to bat each day his bosom heaved a sigh,
While a look of helpless fury shone in mighty Casey's eye.

The lane is long, someone has said, that never turns again,
And fate, though fickle, often gives another chance to men.
And Casey smiled—his rugged face no longer wore a frown;
The pitcher who had started all the trouble came to town.

All Mudville had assembled; ten thousand fans had come
To see the twirler who had put big Casey on the bum;
And when he stepped into the box the multitude went wild.
He doffed his cap in proud disdain—but Casey only smiled.

"Play ball!" the umpire's voice rang out, and then the game began;
But in that throng of thousands there was not a single fan
Who thought that Mudville had a chance; and with the setting sun
Their hopes sank low—the rival team was leading "four to one."

The last half of the ninth came round, with no change in the score;
But when the first man up hit safe the crowd began to roar.
The din increased, the echo of ten thousand shouts was heard
When the pitcher hit the second and gave "four balls" to the third.

Three men on base—nobody out—three runs to tie the game!
A triple meant the highest niche in Mudville's hall of fame;
But here the rally ended and the gloom was deep as night
When the fourth one "fouled to catcher" and the fifth "flew out to right."

CONTINUED ON NEXT PAGE >

A dismal groan in chorus came—a scowl was on each face—
When Casey walked up, bat in hand, and slowly took his place;
His bloodshot eyes in fury gleamed; his teeth were clinched in hate;
He gave his cap a vicious hook and pounded on the plate.

But fame is fleeting as the wind, and glory fades away;
There were no wild and wooly cheers, no glad acclaim this day.
They hissed and groaned and hooted as they clamored, "Strike him out!"
But Casey gave no outward sign that he had heard this shout.

The pitcher smiled and cut one loose; across the plate it spread;
Another hiss, another groan. "Strike one!" the umpire said.
Zip! Like a shot, the second curve broke just below his knee—
"Strike two!" the umpire roared aloud; but Casey made no plea.

No roasting for the umpire now—his was an easy lot;
But here the pitcher whirled again—was that a rifle shot?
A whack! a crack! and out through space the leather pellet flew,
A blot against the distant sky, a speck against the blue.

Above the fence in center field, in rapid whirling flight,
The sphere sailed on; the blot grew dim and then was lost to sight.
Ten thousand hats were thrown in air, ten thousand threw a fit;
But no one ever found the ball that mighty Casey hit.

Oh, somewhere in this favored land dark clouds may hide the sun,
And somewhere bands no longer play and children have no fun;
And somewhere over blighted lives there hangs a heavy pall;
But Mudville hearts are happy now—for Casey hit the ball!

20.
Personal selection

Copy or attach your personal selection choice onto this page.

CERTIFICATE OF COMPLETION

This certifies that

____

has successfully completed the memorization
and presentation requirements for

LEVEL THREE OF

Linguistic Development through Poetry Memorization

____________________ DATE

Listen. Speak. Read. Write. Think!

____________________ SUPERVISOR

Level Four

Poems

Getting Started with Level Four

1. Use the list below to keep track of the poems you are working on, following the methods used in earlier levels. Work at your own pace.
2. To ensure that you maintain the poems from earlier levels, be sure to recite them using the lists provided on the following page.

1 **The Embarrassing Episode of Little Miss Muffet** by Guy Wetmore Carryl
2 **The Tiger** by William Blake
3 **Metaphysics** by Oliver Herford
4 **Lochinvar** by Sir Walter Scott
5 **The Choir Invisible** by George Eliot
6 **The Hand That Rocks the Cradle Is the Hand That Rules the World** by William Ross Wallace
7 **The Maldive Shark** by Herman Melville
8 **The Quality of Mercy** by William Shakespeare
9 **In Flanders Fields** by Dr. John McCrae
10 **Epigram** by Samuel Coleridge
11 **God Save the Flag** by Oliver Wendell Holmes
12 **The Sycophantic Fox and the Gullible Raven** by Guy Wetmore Carryl
13 **A Song from the Suds** by Louisa May Alcott
14 **The Hen** by Oliver Herford
15 **Desiderata** by Max Ehrmann
16 **Woodman, Spare that Tree!** by George P. Morris
17 **Grand Chorus** by John Dryden
18 **An Overworked Elocutionist** by Carolyn Wells
19 **The Hunting of the Dragon** by G.K. Chesterton
20 **Personal selection** (8 lines or shorter): ____________

____

Below, check off the day when you have completed your poetry practice. The letters in the chart refer to the maintenance lists on the next page. The last day of each month is serendipity.* Choose your favorite poems from any list to recite for review.

	1	2	3	4	5	6	7	8	9	10	11	12	13	14	15	16	17	18	19	20	21	22	23	24	25	26	27	28	29	30	31
Aug	A	B	C	D	E	F	G	H	A	B	C	D	E	F	G	H	A	B	C	D	E	F	G	H	A	B	C	D	E	F	★
Sep	G	H	A	B	C	D	E	F	G	H	A	B	C	D	E	F	G	H	A	B	C	D	E	F	G	H	A	B	C	★	
Oct	D	E	F	G	H	A	B	C	D	E	F	G	H	A	B	C	D	E	F	G	H	A	B	C	D	E	F	G	H	A	★
Nov	B	C	D	E	F	G	H	A	B	C	D	E	F	G	H	A	B	C	D	E	F	G	H	A	B	C	D	E	F	★	
Dec	G	H	A	B	C	D	E	F	G	H	A	B	C	D	E	F	G	H	A	B	C	D	E	F	G	H	A	B	C	D	★
Jan	E	F	G	H	A	B	C	D	E	F	G	H	A	B	C	D	E	F	G	H	A	B	C	D	E	F	G	H	A	B	★
Feb	C	D	E	F	G	H	A	B	C	D	E	F	G	H	A	B	C	D	E	F	G	H	A	B	C	D	E	F	★		
Mar	G	H	A	B	C	D	E	F	G	H	A	B	C	D	E	F	G	H	A	B	C	D	E	F	G	H	A	B	C	D	★
Apr	E	F	G	H	A	B	C	D	E	F	G	H	A	B	C	D	E	F	G	H	A	B	C	D	E	F	G	H	A	★	
May	B	C	D	E	F	G	H	A	B	C	D	E	F	G	H	A	B	C	D	E	F	G	H	A	B	C	D	E	F	G	★
Jun	H	A	B	C	D	E	F	G	H	A	B	C	D	E	F	G	H	A	B	C	D	E	F	G	H	A	B	C	D	★	
Jul	E	F	G	H	A	B	C	D	E	F	G	H	A	B	C	D	E	F	G	H	A	B	C	D	E	F	G	H	A	B	★

* Serendipity refers to a pleasant, unexpected surprise or discovery.

Maintaining Earlier Levels

List A

LEVEL ONE

1 Ooey Gooey
9 My Shadow
17 Who Has Seen the Wind?

LEVEL TWO

1 How Doth the Little Crocodile
9 The Height of the Ridiculous

LEVEL THREE

1 A Young Lady Named Bright
9 Grandfather's Clock
17 The Village Blacksmith

List B

LEVEL ONE

2 Celery
10 There Was an Old Person Whose Habits
18 The Eagle

LEVEL TWO

2 At the Seaside
10 The Spider and the Fly

LEVEL THREE

2 A Psalm of Life
10 The Touch of the Master's Hand
18 When I Heard the Learn'd Astronomer

List C

LEVEL ONE

3 The Little Man Who Wasn't There
11 Jonathan Bing
19 The Swan and the Goose

LEVEL TWO

3 Rebecca, Who Slammed Doors for Fun
11 Trees

LEVEL THREE

3 The Road Not Taken
11 The Unknown Soldier
19 Casey's Revenge

List D

LEVEL ONE

4 The Vulture
12 Whole Duty of Children
20 Personal Selection:

____

LEVEL TWO

4 Fog
12 Ballad of the Tempest

LEVEL THREE

4 O Captain! My Captain!
12 The Pessimist
20 Personal Selection:

____

List E

LEVEL ONE

5 After the Party
13 Godfrey Gordon Gustavus Gore

LEVEL TWO

5 Some One
13 The Charge of the Light Brigade
17 Conscience and Remorse

LEVEL THREE

5 Matilda, Who Told Lies
13 The Fool's Prayer

List F

LEVEL ONE

6 Singing Time
14 My Gift

LEVEL TWO

6 The Duke of Plaza-Toro
14 Sea Fever
18 Stopping by Woods on a Snowy Evening

LEVEL THREE

6 Scintillate, Scintillate
14 Casey at the Bat

List G

LEVEL ONE

7 The Yak
15 The Swing

LEVEL TWO

7 God and the Soldier
15 Shoes
19 Project

LEVEL THREE

7 What I Live For
15 He Wishes for the Cloths of Heaven

List H

LEVEL ONE

8 The Ingenious Little Old Man
16 Persevere

LEVEL TWO

8 Jabberwocky
16 The Glove and the Lions
20 Personal Selection:

____

LEVEL THREE

8 Courage
16 The Destruction of Sennacherib

1.

The Embarrassing Episode of Little Miss Muffet

BY GUY WETMORE CARRYL

Little Miss Muffet discovered a tuffet,
(Which never occurred to the rest of us)
and, as 'twas a June day, and just about noonday,
She wanted to eat—like the best of us:
Her diet was whey, and I hasten to say
It is wholesome and people grow fat on it.
The spot being lonely, the lady not only
Discovered the tuffet, but sat on it.

A rivulet gabbled beside her and babbled,
As rivulets always are thought to do,
And dragonflies sported around and cavorted,
As poets say dragonflies ought to do;
When, glancing aside for a moment, she spied
A horrible sight that brought fear to her,
A hideous spider was sitting beside her,
And most unavoidably near to her!

Albeit unsightly, this creature politely
Said: "Madam, I earnestly vow to you,
I'm penitent that I did not bring my hat. I
Should otherwise certainly bow to you."
Though anxious to please, he was so ill at ease
That he lost all his sense of propriety,
And grew so inept that he clumsily stept
In her plate—which is barred in Society.

This curious error completed her terror;
She shuddered, and growing much paler, not
Only left tuffet, but dealt him a buffet
Which doubled him up in a sailor knot.
It should be explained that at this he was pained:
He cried: "I have vexed you, no doubt of it!
Your fist's like a truncheon." "You're still in my luncheon,"
Was all that she answered. "Get out of it!"

And the Moral is this: Be it madam or miss
To whom you have something to say,
You are only absurd when you get in the curd
But you're rude when you get in the whey!

2.
The Tiger

BY WILLIAM BLAKE

Tiger, tiger, burning bright,
In the forests of the night,
What immortal hand or eye
Could frame thy fearful symmetry?

In what distant deeps or skies
Burnt the fire of thine eyes?
On what wings dare he aspire?
What the hand dare seize the fire?

And what shoulder, and what art,
Could twist the sinews of thy heart?
And when thy heart began to beat,
What dread hand and what dread feet?

What the hammer? What the chain?
In what furnace was thy brain?
What the anvil? What dread grasp
Dare its deadly terrors clasp?

When the stars threw down their spears,
And water'd heaven with their tears,
Did He smile His work to see?
Did He who made the Lamb, make thee?

Tiger, tiger, burning bright,
In the forests of the night,
What immortal hand or eye
Dare frame thy fearful symmetry?

3.
Metaphysics

BY OLIVER HERFORD

Why and Wherefore set out one day
To hunt for a wild Negation.
They agreed to meet at a cool retreat
On the Point of Interrogation.

But the night was dark and they missed their mark,
And, driven well-nigh to distraction,
They lost their ways in a murky maze
Of utter abstruse abstraction.

Then they took a boat and were soon afloat
On a Sea of Speculation,
But the sea grew rough, and their boat, though tough,
Was split into an Equation.

As they floundered about in the Waves of Doubt
Rose a fearful Hypothesis,
Who gibbered with glee as they sank in the sea,
And the last they saw was this:

On a rock-bound Reef of Unbelief
There sat the wild Negation;
Then they sank once more and were washed ashore
At the Point of Interrogation.

4.
Lochinvar

BY SIR WALTER SCOTT

O, young Lochinvar is come out of the west,
Through all the wide Border his steed was the best,
And save his good broadsword he weapons had none;
He rode all unarmed, and he rode all alone.
So faithful in love, and so dauntless in war,
There never was knight like the young Lochinvar.

He stayed not for brake, and he stopped not for stone,
He swam the Eske river where ford there was none;
But, ere he alighted at Netherby gate,
The bride had consented, the gallant came late:
For a laggard in love, and a dastard in war,
Was to wed the fair Ellen of brave Lochinvar.

So boldly he entered the Netherby hall,
Among bride's-men and kinsmen, and brothers and all;
Then spoke the bride's father, his hand on his sword
(For the poor craven bridegroom said never a word),
"O come ye in peace here, or come ye in war,
Or to dance at our bridal, young Lord Lochinvar?"

"I long wooed your daughter, my suit you denied;—
Love swells like the Solway, but ebbs like its tide—
And now I am come, with this lost love of mine,
To lead but one measure, drink one cup of wine.
There are maidens in Scotland more lovely by far,
That would gladly be bride to the young Lochinvar."

The bride kissed the goblet; the knight took it up,
He quaffed off the wine, and he threw down the cup,
She looked down to blush, and she looked up to sigh,
With a smile on her lips and a tear in her eye.
He took her soft hand, ere her mother could bar,—
"Now tread we a measure!" said young Lochinvar.

CONTINUED ON NEXT PAGE ›

So stately his form, and so lovely her face,
That never a hall such a galliard did grace;
While her mother did fret, and her father did fume,
And the bridegroom stood dangling his bonnet and plume;
And the bride-maidens whispered, "'Twere better by far
To have matched our fair cousin with young Lochinvar."

One touch to her hand, and one word in her ear,
When they reached the hall door, and the charger stood near;
So light to the croupe the fair lady he swung,
So light to the saddle before her he sprung!
"She is won! We are gone, over bank, bush, and scaur;
They'll have fleet steeds that follow," quoth young Lochinvar.

There was mounting 'mong Graemes of the Netherby clan;
Forsters, Fenwicks, and Musgraves, they rode and they ran;
There was racing, and chasing, on Cannobie Lee,
But the lost bride of Netherby ne'er did they see.
So daring in love, and so dauntless in war,
Have ye e'er heard of gallant like young Lochinvar?

5.
The Choir Invisible

BY GEORGE ELIOT

O may I join the choir invisible
Of those immortal dead who live again
In minds made better by their presence; live
In pulses stirred to generosity,
In deeds of daring rectitude, in scorn
Of miserable aims that end with self,
In thoughts sublime that pierce the night like stars,
And with their mild persistence urge men's minds
To vaster issues.

...

May I reach
That purest heaven—be to other souls
The cup of strength in some great agony,
Enkindle generous ardor, feed pure love,
Beget the smiles that have no cruelty,
Be the sweet presence of a good diffused,
And in diffusion ever more intense!
So shall I join the choir invisible,
Whose music is the gladness of the world.

6.
The Hand That Rocks the Cradle Is the Hand That Rules the World

BY WILLIAM ROSS WALLACE

Blessings on the hand of woman!
Angels guard its strength and grace,
In the palace, cottage, hovel,
Oh, no matter where the place;
Would that never storms assailed it,
Rainbows ever gently curled;
For the hand that rocks the cradle
Is the hand that rules the world.

Infancy's the tender fountain,
Power may with beauty flow,
Mother's first to guide the streamlets,
From them souls unresting grow—
Grow on for the good or evil,
Sunshine streamed or evil hurled;
For the hand that rocks the cradle
Is the hand that rules the world.

Woman, how divine your mission
Here upon our natal sod!
Keep, oh, keep the young heart open
Always to the breath of God!
All true trophies of the ages
Are from mother-love impearled;
For the hand that rocks the cradle
Is the hand that rules the world.

Blessings on the hand of woman!
Fathers, sons, and daughters cry,
And the sacred song is mingled
With the worship in the sky—
Mingles where no tempest darkens,
Rainbows evermore are hurled;
For the hand that rocks the cradle
Is the hand that rules the world.

7.
The Maldive Shark

BY HERMAN MELVILLE

About the Shark, phlegmatical one,
Pale sot of the Maldive sea,
The sleek little pilot-fish, azure and slim,
How alert in attendance be.
From his saw-pit of mouth, from his charnel of maw,
They have nothing of harm to dread,
But liquidly glide on his ghastly flank
Or before his Gorgonian head;
Or lurk in the port of serrated teeth
In white triple tiers of glittering gates,
And there find a haven when peril's abroad,
An asylum in jaws of the Fates!
They are friends; and friendly they guide him to prey,
Yet never partake of the treat—
Eyes and brains to the dotard lethargic and dull,
Pale ravener of horrible meat.

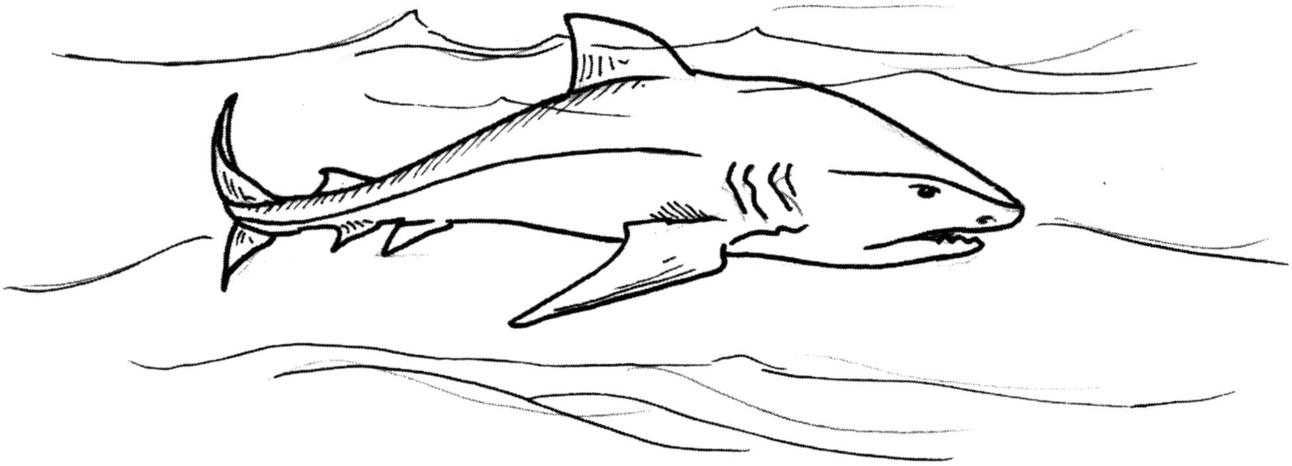

8.

The Quality of Mercy

from *The Merchant of Venice*

BY WILLIAM SHAKESPEARE

The quality of mercy is not strain'd.
It droppeth as the gentle rain from heaven
Upon the place beneath. It is twice blest:
It blesseth him that gives, and him that takes.
'Tis mightiest in the mightiest; it becomes
The throned monarch better than his crown.
His scepter shows the force of temporal power,
The attribute to awe and majesty,
Wherein doth sit the dread and fear of kings;
But mercy is above this sceptered sway;
It is enthroned in the hearts of kings;
It is an attribute to God himself;
And earthly power doth then show likest God's
When mercy seasons justice.

9.
In Flanders Fields

BY DR. JOHN McCRAE

In Flanders fields the poppies blow
Between the crosses, row on row,
That marked our place; and in the sky
The larks, still bravely singing, fly
Scarce heard amid the guns below.

We are the dead. Short days ago
We lived, felt dawn, saw sunset glow,
Loved and were loved, and now we lie
  In Flanders fields.

Take up our quarrel with the foe:
To you from failing hands we throw the torch;
Be yours to hold it high.
If ye break faith with us who die
We shall not sleep, though poppies grow
  In Flanders fields.

10.
Epigram

BY SAMUEL COLERIDGE

Sir, I admit your general rule,
That every poet is a fool,
But you yourself may serve to show it,
That every fool is not a poet.

11.
God Save the Flag

BY OLIVER WENDELL HOLMES

Washed in the blood of the brave and the blooming,
Snatched from the altars of insolent foes,
Burning with star-fires, but never consuming,
Flash its broad ribbons of lily and rose.

Vainly the prophets of Baal would rend it,
Vainly his worshippers pray for its fall;
Thousands have died for it, millions defend it,
Emblem of justice and mercy to all;

Justice that reddens the sky with her terrors,
Mercy that comes with her white-handed train,
Soothing all passions, redeeming all errors,
Sheathing the sabre and breaking the chain.

Borne on the deluge of all usurpations,
Drifted our Ark o'er the desolate seas,
Bearing the rainbow of hope to the nations,
Torn from the storm-cloud and flung to the breeze!

God bless the Flag and its loyal defenders,
While its broad folds o'er the battle-field wave,
Till the dim star-wreath rekindle its splendors,
Washed from its stains in the blood of the brave!

12.
The Sycophantic Fox and the Gullible Raven

BY GUY WETMORE CARRYL

A raven sat upon a tree,
And not a word he spoke, for
His beak contained a piece of Brie,
Or, maybe, it was Roquefort:
We'll make it any kind you please—
At all events, it was a cheese.

Beneath the tree's umbrageous limb
A hungry fox sat smiling;
He saw the raven watching him,
And spoke in words beguiling:
"*J'admire*," said he, "*ton beau plumage*,"
(The which was simply persiflage).

Two things there are, no doubt you know,
To which a fox is used,—
A rooster that is bound to crow,
A crow that's bound to roost,
And whichsoever he espies
He tells the most unblushing lies.

"Sweet fowl," he said, "I understand
You're more than merely natty:
I hear you sing to beat the band
And Adelina Patti.
Pray render with your liquid tongue
A bit from 'Götterdämmerung!'"

This subtle speech was aimed to please
The crow, and it succeeded;
He thought no bird in all the trees
Could sing as well as he did.
In flattery completely doused,
He gave the "Jewel Song" from "Faust."

But gravitation's law, of course,
As Isaac Newton showed it,
Exerted on the cheese its force,
And elsewhere soon bestowed it.
In fact, there is no need to tell
What happened when to earth it fell.

I blush to add that when the bird
Took in the situation,
He said one brief, emphatic word,
Unfit for publication.
The fox was greatly startled, but
He only sighed and answered "Tut!"

The moral is: A fox is bound
To be a shameless sinner.
And also: When the cheese comes round
You know it's after dinner.
But (what is only known to few)
The fox is after dinner, too.

13.
A Song from the Suds

BY LOUISA MAY ALCOTT

Queen of my tub, I merrily sing,
While the white foam rises high,
And sturdily wash, and rinse, and wring,
And fasten the clothes to dry;
Then out in the free fresh air they swing,
Under the sunny sky.

I wish we could wash from our hearts and our souls
The stains of the week away,
And let water and air by their magic make
Ourselves as pure as they;
Then on the earth there would be indeed
A glorious washing day!

Along the path of a useful life
Will heart's-ease ever bloom;
The busy mind has no time to think
Of sorrow, or care, or gloom;
And anxious thoughts may be swept away
As we busily wield a broom.

I am glad a task to me is given
To labor at day by day;
For it brings me health, and strength, and hope,
And I cheerfully learn to say—
"Head, you may think; heart, you may feel;
But hand, you shall work alway!"

14.
The Hen

BY OLIVER HERFORD

Alas, my Child, where is the Pen
That can do Justice to the Hen?

Like Royalty, She goes her way,
Laying foundations every day,

Though not for Public Buildings, yet
For Custard, Cake and Omelette.

Or if too Old for such a use
They have their Fling at some Abuse,

As when to Censure Plays Unfit
Upon the Stage they make a Hit,

Or at elections Seal the Fate
Of an Obnoxious Candidate.

No wonder, Child, we prize the Hen,
Whose Egg is mightier than the Pen.

15.
Desiderata

BY MAX EHRMANN

Go placidly amid the noise and the haste,
and remember what peace there may be in silence.
As far as possible, without surrender, be on good terms with all persons.
Speak your truth quietly and clearly, and listen to others,
even to the dull and the ignorant; they too have their story.
Avoid loud and aggressive persons; they are vexatious to the spirit.
If you compare yourself with others, you may become vain or bitter,
for always there will be greater and lesser persons than yourself.

Enjoy your achievements as well as your plans.
Keep interested in your own career, however humble;
it is a real possession in the changing fortunes of time.
Exercise caution in your business affairs, for the world is full of trickery.
But let this not blind you to what virtue there is;
many persons strive for high ideals, and everywhere life is full of heroism.

Be yourself.
Especially, do not feign affection.
Neither be cynical about love,
for in the face of all aridity and disenchantment, it is as perennial as the grass.

Take kindly the counsel of the years, gracefully surrendering the things of youth.
Nurture strength of spirit to shield you in sudden misfortune.
But do not distress yourself with dark imaginings.
Many fears are born of fatigue and loneliness.
Beyond a wholesome discipline, be gentle with yourself.

You are a child of the universe no less than the trees and the stars;
you have a right to be here.
And whether or not it is clear to you,
no doubt the universe is unfolding as it should.

Therefore be at peace with God, whatever you conceive Him to be.
And whatever your labors and aspirations,
in the noisy confusion of life, keep peace in your soul.
With all its sham, drudgery, and broken dreams, it is still a beautiful world.
Be cheerful. Strive to be happy.

16.
Woodman, Spare that Tree!

BY GEORGE P. MORRIS

Woodman, spare that tree!
  Touch not a single bough!
In youth it sheltered me,
  And I'll protect it now.
'Twas my forefather's hand
  That placed it near his cot;
There, woodman, let it stand,
  Thy axe shall harm it not!

That old familiar tree,
  Whose glory and renown
Are spread o'er land and sea,
  And wouldst thou hew it down?
Woodman, forbear thy stroke!
  Cut not its earth-bound ties;
O, spare that aged oak,
  Now towering to the skies!

When but an idle boy
  I sought its grateful shade;
In all their gushing joy
  Here too my sisters played.
My mother kissed me here;
  My father pressed my hand—
Forgive this foolish tear,
  But let that old oak stand!

My heart-strings round thee cling,
  Close as thy bark, old friend!
Here shall the wild-bird sing,
  And still thy branches bend.
Old tree! The storm still brave!
  And woodman, leave the spot;
While I've a hand to save,
  Thy axe shall hurt it not.

17.
Grand Chorus

BY JOHN DRYDEN

As from the power of sacred lays
The spheres begin to move,
And sung to the Creator's praise
To all the blessed above;
So when the last and dreadful hour
This crumbling pageant shall devour,
The trumpet shall be heard on high,
The dead shall live, the living die,
And music shall untune the sky.

18.
An Overworked Elocutionist

BY CAROLYN WELLS

Once there was a little boy whose name was Robert Reese;
And every Friday afternoon he had to speak a piece.
So many poems thus he learned, that soon he had a store
Of recitations in his head and still kept learning more.

And now this is what happened: He was called upon one week
And totally forgot the piece he was about to speak.
His brain he cudgeled. Not a word remained within his head!
And so he spoke at random, and this is what he said:

"My beautiful, my beautiful, who standest proudly by,
It was the schooner Hesperus—the breaking waves dashed high!
Why is this Forum crowded? What means this stir in Rome!
Under a spreading chestnut tree, there is no place like home!

When freedom from her mountain height cried, 'Twinkle, little star,'
Shoot if you must this old gray head, King Henry of Navarre!
Roll on, thou deep and dark blue castled crag of Drachenfels,
My name is Norval, on the Grampian Hills, ring out, wild bells!

If you're waking, call me early. To be or not to be,
The curfew must not ring tonight! Oh, woodman, spare that tree!
Charge, Chester, charge! On, Stanley, on! And let who will be clever!
The boy stood on the burning deck, but I go on forever!"

His elocution was superb, his voice and gestures fine;
His schoolmates all applauded as he finished the last line.
"I see it doesn't matter," Robert thought, "what words I say,
So long as I declaim with oratorical display."

19.
The Hunting of the Dragon

BY G.K. CHESTERTON

When we went hunting the Dragon
In the days when we were young,
We tossed the bright world
over our shoulder
As bugle and baldrick slung;
Never was world so wild and fair
As what went by on the wind,

Never such fields of paradise
As the fields we left behind;
For this is the best of a rest for men
That men should rise and ride
Making a flying fairyland
Of market and country-side,
Wings on the cottage,
wings on the wood,
Wings upon pot and pan,
For the hunting of the Dragon
That is the life of a man.

For men grow weary of fairyland
When the Dragon is a dream,
And tire of the talking bird in the tree,
The singing fish in the stream;
And the wandering stars grow stale,
grow stale,
And the wonder is stiff with scorn;
For this is the honour of fairyland
And the following of the horn;

Beauty on beauty called us back
When we could rise and ride,
And a woman looked
out of every window
As wonderful as a bride;
And the tavern-sign as a tabard blazed,
And the children cheered and ran,
For the love of the hate of the Dragon
That is the pride of a man.

The sages called him a shadow
And the light went out of the sun;
And the wise men told us
that all was well
And all was weary and one;
And then, and then, in the quiet garden,
With never a weed to kill,
We knew that his shining tail had shone
In the white road over the hill;
We knew that the clouds were flakes of flame,
We knew that the sunset fire
Was red with the blood of the Dragon
Whose death is the world's desire.

For the horn was blown
in the heart of the night
That men should rise and ride,
Keeping the tryst of a terrible jest
Never for long untried;
Drinking a dreadful blood for wine,
Never in cup or can,
The death of a deathless Dragon,
That is the life of a man.

20.
Personal selection

Copy or attach your personal selection choice onto this page.

CERTIFICATE OF COMPLETION

This certifies that

____

has successfully completed the memorization
and presentation requirements for

LEVEL FOUR OF
Linguistic Development through Poetry Memorization

Listen. Speak. Read. Write. Think!

______________ DATE

______________ SUPERVISOR

Level Five

Speeches

Getting Started with Level Five

1. Highlight the first speech and recite it daily, using the audio CD.
2. Practice reciting it daily, with or without the audio help.
3. When you have memorized the first speech, highlight the second speech and begin memorizing it. In this way, continue to work through the list of speeches.
4. Practice all the highlighted speeches every day so that you will master them.
5. The last day of each month is serendipity.* On that day recite your favorite poems and speeches.

1 **Socrates' Apology** by Plato
2 **First Oration Against Catiline** by Cicero
3 **On the Eve of the Battle with the Spanish Armada** by Elizabeth I
4 **St. Crispin's Day Speech** by William Shakespeare
5 **Friends, Romans, Countrymen** by William Shakespeare
6 **Give Me Liberty** by Patrick Henry
7 **Declaration of Independence Excerpt**
8 **Preamble to the Constitution of the United States of America**
9 **1789 Abolition Speech** by William Wilberforce
10 **What to the Slave Is the Fourth of July?** by Frederick Douglass
11 **Opening Lines of *A Tale of Two Cities*** by Charles Dickens
12 **The Gettysburg Address** by Abraham Lincoln
13 **Address at a Gathering of Americans in London, July 4, 1872 (excerpted)** by Mark Twain
14 **Excerpts from "The Strenuous Life"** by Theodore Roosevelt
15 **The King's Speech** by King George VI
16 **We Shall Fight on the Beaches** by Winston Churchill
17 **For We Let Our Young Men and Women Go Out Unarmed** by Dorothy Sayers
18 **Anyway** attributed to Mother Teresa
19 **Brandenburg Gate Speech** by Ronald Reagan
20 **Freedom from Fear Speech** by Aung San Suu Kyi

Below, check off the day when you have recited all of the highlighted speeches.

	1	2	3	4	5	6	7	8	9	10	11	12	13	14	15	16	17	18	19	20	21	22	23	24	25	26	27	28	29	30	31
Aug																															
Sep																															
Oct																															
Nov																															
Dec																															
Jan																															
Feb																															
Mar																															
Apr																															
May																															
Jun																															
Jul																															

* Serendipity refers to a pleasant, unexpected surprise or discovery.

1.
Socrates' Apology EXCERPT

BY PLATO (428–348 BC)

Plato was a student of Socrates and taught Aristotle. He founded the Academy Athens, which laid the foundation for universities. Plato wrote "Socrates' Apology" shortly after Socrates' execution for "refusing to recognize the gods recognized by the state and introducing other, new divinities. He is also guilty of corrupting the youth." Below is an excerpt of the work.

This speech is an excerpt of a longer work.

Since this is an ancient work, no original copies remain. Plato's work has been copied through the ages, and as a result not all copies match. Moreover, the original was written in ancient Greek and thus needed to be translated into English. The translation of the excerpt for this book was done by Benjamin Jowett in 1871 because it is considered the most readable of the available translations. The spelling is British standard.

Additional information about the author and this work can be found on literary websites, such as Sparknotes.com.

Socrates' Apology **from Plato translated from the Greek by Benjamin Jowett**

The word *apology* in the title means *defense.*

For the fear of death is indeed the pretence of wisdom, and not real wisdom, being a pretence of knowing the unknown; and no one knows whether death, which men in their fear apprehend to be the greatest evil, may not be the greatest good. Is not this ignorance of a disgraceful sort, the ignorance which is the conceit that a man knows what he does not know? And in this respect only I believe myself to differ from men in general, and may perhaps claim to be wiser than they are: that whereas I know but little of the world below, I do not suppose that I know, but I do know that injustice and disobedience to a better, whether god or man, is evil and dishonourable, and I will never fear or avoid a possible good rather than a certain evil.

Anytus /en-ē-tes/ was one of the prosecutors in the trial of Socrates.

And therefore if you let me go now, and are not convinced by Anytus, who said that since I had been prosecuted I must be put to death (or if not that I ought never to have been prosecuted at all); and that if I escape now, your sons will all be utterly ruined by listening to my words—if you say to me, Socrates, this time we will not mind Anytus, and you shall be let off, but upon one condition, that you are not to enquire and speculate in this way anymore, and that if you are caught doing so again you shall die—if this was the condition on which you let me go, I should reply: Men of Athens, I honour and love you; but I shall obey god rather than you, and while I have life and strength I shall never cease from the practice and teaching of philosophy, exhorting anyone whom I meet and saying

Plato and Socrates were Greek philosophers who lived in a society where the Greek gods were worshipped.

to him after my manner: You, my friend—a citizen of the great and mighty and wise city of Athens—are you not ashamed of heaping up the greatest amount of money and honour and reputation, and caring so little about wisdom and truth and the greatest improvement of the soul, which you never regard or heed at all? And if the person with whom I am arguing, says: Yes, but I do care, then I do not leave him or let him go at once; but I proceed to interrogate and examine and cross-examine him, and if I think that he has no virtue in him, but only says that he has, I reproach him with undervaluing the greater, and overvaluing the less.

And I shall repeat the same words to everyone whom I meet, young and old, citizen and alien, but especially to the citizens, inasmuch as they are my brethren. For know that this is the command of god; and I believe that no greater good has ever happened in the state than my service to the god. For I do nothing but go about persuading you all, old and young alike, not to take thought for your persons or your properties, but first and chiefly to care about the greatest improvement of the soul. I tell you that virtue is not given by money, but that from virtue comes money and every other good of man, public as well as private. This is my teaching, and if this is the doctrine which corrupts the youth, I am a mischievous person. But if anyone says that this is not my teaching, he is speaking an untruth. Wherefore, O men of Athens, I say to you, do as Anytus bids or not as Anytus bids, and either acquit me or not; but whichever you do, understand that I shall never alter my ways, not even if I have to die many times.

2.
First Oration Against Catiline

BY CICERO (106–43 BC)

Catiline was a man of high social standing and noble ancestry who lacked riches. He sought to be elected to the consulship of Rome, but failed at every turn. When he lost to Cicero, a newcomer to the senate, Catiline devised a plot with fellow aristocrats and discontented veterans to overthrow the Roman Republic. The plot was exposed. When Catiline arrived in the senate on November 8, 63 BC, Cicero spoke out against him. His speech became known as the first Catilinarian. The excerpt below was translated from the Latin by Charles Duke Yonge in 1856.

For more on the conspiracy of Catiline, visit IEW.com/LDP-info.

Cicero, excerpt from the First Oration Against Catiline translated by Charles Duke Yonge

We have now for a long time, O conscript fathers, lived among these dangers and machinations of conspiracy; but somehow or other, the ripeness of all wickedness, and of this long-standing madness and audacity, has come to a head at the time of my consulship. But if this man alone is removed from this piratical crew, we may appear, perhaps, for a short time relieved from fear and anxiety, but the danger will settle down and lie hid in the veins and bowels of the republic. As it often happens that men afflicted with a severe disease, when they are tortured with heat and fever, if they drink cold water, seem at first to be relieved, but afterward suffer more and more severely; so this disease which is in the republic, if relieved by the punishment of this man, will only get worse and worse, as the rest will be still alive.

machinations: secret plots to accomplish an evil end

consulship: the highest level of public office. Two consuls were elected each year, holding office for one year and wielding great power.

Wherefore, O conscript fathers, let the worthless be gone; let them separate themselves from the good; let them collect in one place; let them, as I have often said before, be separated from us by a wall; let them cease to plot against the consul in his own house; to surround the tribunal of the city pretor, to besiege the senate-house with swords, to prepare brands and torches to burn the city—let it, in short, be written on the brow of every citizen, what his sentiments are about the republic. I promise you this, O conscript fathers, that there shall be so much diligence in us the consuls, so much authority in you, so much virtue in the Roman knights, so much unanimity in all good men that you shall see everything made plain and manifest by the departure of Catiline—everything checked and punished.

To gain power, Catiline devised a plan to take over the city of Rome. In addition to plotting Cicero's death, Catiline prepared an army to march on Rome. Swords were held in a house, and fellow conspirators were to set fires around the city when the army approached.

With these omens, O Catiline, be gone to your impious and nefarious war, to the great safety of the republic, to your own misfortune and injury, and to the destruction of those who have joined themselves to you in every wickedness and

impious: lack of respect for a deity

nefarious: evil or immoral

atrocity. Then do you, O Jupiter, who were consecrated by Romulus with the same auspices as this city, whom we rightly call the stay of this city and empire, repel this man and his companions from your altars and from the other temples—from the houses and walls of the city, from the lives and fortunes of all the citizens—and overwhelm all the enemies of good men: the foes of the republic, the robbers of Italy, men bound together by a treaty and infamous alliance of crimes, dead and alive—with eternal punishments.

Jupiter: the chief Roman god who was god of the state and its welfare and laws

Romulus: son of Mars and legendary founder of Rome

3.

On the Eve of the Battle with the Spanish Armada

BY ELIZABETH I (1533–1603)

One of the most famous events in English history is the defeat of the Spanish Armada. In 1585 King Philip II began to prepare a fleet that would invade England. Consisting of over one hundred ships, the Spanish Armada planned to sail along the English Channel and meet forces from the Netherlands, setting sail towards England. However, the weather hindered the Spanish Armada, making it possible for the English to scatter the fleet with superior ships and tactics.

While the English navy battled Spain at sea, English soldiers gathered at Tilbury, ready to fight the Spanish when they landed. Dressed in white with silver armor, Queen Elizabeth addressed her soldiers, delivering what may be her most famous speech of all.

Although there are several versions of the speech, the most famous text was found in a letter from Leonel Sharp to the Duke of Buckingham.

Elizabeth I, Queen of England, on the eve of the battle with the Spanish Armada

Elizabeth I is pronounced "Elizabeth the First."

My loving people, we have been persuaded by some that are careful of our safety, to take heed how we commit ourselves to armed multitudes for fear of treachery; but, I do assure you, I do not desire to live to distrust my faithful and loving people.

Let tyrants fear; I have always so behaved myself, that under God I have placed my chiefest strength and safeguard in the loyal hearts and good will of my subjects; and, therefore, I am come amongst you as you see at this time, not for my recreation and disport, but being resolved, in the midst and heat of the battle, to live or die amongst you all—to lay down for my God, and for my kingdoms, and for my people, my honor and my blood even in the dust.

I know I have the body of a weak, feeble woman; but I have the heart and stomach of a king—and of a King of England too, and think foul scorn that Parma or Spain, or any prince of Europe, should dare to invade the borders of my realm; to which, rather than any dishonor should grow by me, I myself will take up arms—I myself will be your general, judge, and rewarder of every one of your virtues in the field.

Parma: The Duke of Parma commanded the Netherlands' army, which never did connect with the Spanish Armada as planned.

I know already, for your forwardness, you have deserved rewards and crowns, and, we do assure you, on the word of a prince, they shall be duly paid you. For the meantime, my Lieutenant General Leicester shall be in my stead, than whom never prince commanded a more noble or worthy subject; not doubting but by your obedience to my General, by your concord in the camp, and your valor in the field, we shall shortly have a famous victory over these enemies of my God, of my kingdom and of my people.

Leicester: Robert Dudley, Earl of Leicester and close friend of the queen, commanded the English land forces. He died unexpectedly just a month after the famous battle.

4.
St. Crispin's Day Speech
from *Henry V*

BY WILLIAM SHAKESPEARE (1564–1616)

In addition to comedies and tragedies, William Shakespeare wrote historical plays.

The play leads up to the famous Battle of Agincourt between England and France, fought on St. Crispin's Day in 1415. The English were hopelessly outnumbered, five to one. As King Henry enters, the Earl of Westmoreland laments, "Oh that we now had here but one ten thousand of those men in England that do no work today!" This speech below is part of Henry's reply, made not only to Westmoreland, but to all his men. Despite the odds, England won the battle.

Written in 1599, *Henry V* is the fourth play in a four-part series following the rise of the House of Lancaster. For more about the play, visit sparknotes.com or shmoop.com.

From Shakespeare's *Henry V*

No, my fair cousin; If we are mark'd to die, we are
enow
To do our country loss; and if to live,
The fewer men, the greater share of honour.
God's will! I pray thee, wish not one man more.
By Jove, I am not covetous for gold,
Nor care I who doth feed upon my cost;
It yearns me not if men my garments wear;
Such outward things dwell not in my desires.
But if it be a sin to covet honour,
I am the most offending soul alive.

This day is call'd the feast of Crispian.
He that outlives this day, and comes safe home,
Will stand a tip-toe when this day is nam'd,
And rouse him at the name of Crispian.
He that shall live this day, and see old age,
Will yearly on the vigil feast his neighbours,
And say "To-morrow is Saint Crispian."
Then will he strip his sleeve and show his scars,
And say "These wounds I had on Crispian's day."
Old men forget; yet all shall be forgot,
But he'll remember, with advantages,
What feats he did that day. Then shall our names,
Familiar in his mouth as household words—
Harry the King, Bedford and Exeter,
Warwick and Talbot, Salisbury and Gloucester—
Be in their flowing cups freshly rememb'red.
This story shall the good man teach his son;
And Crispin Crispian shall ne'er go by,
From this day to the ending of the world,
But we in it shall be remembered—
We few, we happy few, we band of brothers;
For he to-day that sheds his blood with me
Shall be my brother; be he ne'er so vile,
This day shall gentle his condition;
And gentlemen in England now-a-bed
Shall think themselves accurs'd they were not here,
And hold their manhoods cheap whiles any speaks
That fought with us upon Saint Crispin's day.

Henry V is pronounced "Henry the Fifth."

enow: enough

Feast of Crispian: St. Crispin's Day, October 25, is the feast day of Saints Crispin and Crispinian, twins who were martyred in 286. Interestingly, other famous battles were fought on this date, most notably the Battle of Balaclava, made famous in Tennyson's "The Charge of the Light Brigade."

Bedford and Gloucester were two of Henry's three younger brothers. Exeter, Westmoreland, Salisbury, and Warwick were trusted advisors to the king. Exeter was also Henry's uncle. Talbot, Earl of Shrewsbury was a famous commander serving Henry IV, V, and VI.

5. Friends, Romans, Countrymen

from *Julius Caesar*

BY WILLIAM SHAKESPEARE (1564–1616)

Shakespeare wrote Julius Caesar in 1599 and based the tragedy on true events from Roman history. The play opens with Julius Caesar's triumphant return from battle where he defeated the sons of Pompey, who had tried to overthrow Caesar. Other Roman senators are worried that Caesar might gain absolute power. They end up plotting Caesar's death and carrying out the assassination at the Capitol on the Ides of March.

Although Antony, one of Caesar's friends, says he is committed to the conspirators, he determines to speak at Caesar's funeral and incite the crowd against the men who murdered him. Brutus speaks first and the crowd is sympathetic to him. But then Antony shows up with Caesar's body and gives this impassioned speech, using reverse psychology to move the crowd to avenge Caesar's death.

From Shakespeare's *Julius Caesar*

Friends, Romans, countrymen, lend me your ears;
I come to bury Caesar, not to praise him.
The evil that men do lives after them;
The good is oft interred with their bones;
So let it be with Caesar. The noble Brutus
Hath told you Caesar was ambitious:
If it were so, it was a grievous fault,
And grievously hath Caesar answer'd it.

Here, under leave of Brutus and the rest—
For Brutus is an honourable man;
So are they all, all honourable men—
Come I to speak in Caesar's funeral.
He was my friend, faithful and just to me:
But Brutus says he was ambitious;
And Brutus is an honourable man.
He hath brought many captives home to Rome
Whose ransoms did the general coffers fill:
Did this in Caesar seem ambitious?
When that the poor have cried, Caesar hath wept:
Ambition should be made of sterner stuff:
Yet Brutus says he was ambitious;
And Brutus is an honourable man.
You all did see that on the Lupercal
I thrice presented him a kingly crown,
Which he did thrice refuse: was this ambition?
Yet Brutus says he was ambitious;
And, sure, he is an honourable man.

I speak not to disprove what Brutus spoke,
But here I am to speak what I do know.
You all did love him once, not without cause:
What cause withholds you then, to mourn for him?
O judgment! thou art fled to brutish beasts,
And men have lost their reason. Bear with me;
My heart is in the coffin there with Caesar,
And I must pause till it come back to me.

Lupercal: short for Lupercalia, an annual Roman holiday in mid-February meant to purify the city from evil spirits and promote health and fertility

6.
Give Me Liberty

BY PATRICK HENRY (1736–1799)

In March of 1775, delegates to the House of Burgess met at St. John's Church in Richmond, Virginia, to discuss whether or not to arm the colony of Virginia should the British army march against them. On the fourth day of the meeting, March 23, Henry rose to deliver his famous speech, excerpted below. Although members of the House were reluctant to oppose their mother country, Henry's persuasive words inspired the delegates to support the cause of freedom.

Sadly, Henry's actual speech was never written down. It was first published by William Wirt in 1805 in his biography of Patrick Henry. The speech as written exhibits a variety of rhetorical devices and strategies. Visit IEW.com/LDP-info for a link to a site with examples of these techniques.

From a speech by Patrick Henry
March 23, 1775

The battle, sir, is not to the strong alone; it is to the vigilant, the active, the brave. Besides, sir, we have no election. If we were base enough to desire it, it is now too late to retire from the contest. There is no retreat but in submission and slavery! Our chains are forged! Their clanking may be heard on the plains of Boston! The war is inevitable—and let it come! I repeat it, sir, let it come!

It is in vain, sir, to extenuate the matter. Gentlemen may cry, "Peace! Peace!"—but there is no peace. The war is actually begun! The next gale that sweeps from the north will bring to our ears the clash of resounding arms! Our brethren are already in the field! Why stand we here idle? What is it that gentlemen wish? What would they have? Is life so dear, or peace so sweet, as to be purchased at the price of chains and slavery? Forbid it, Almighty God! I know not what course others may take; but as for me, give me liberty, or give me death!

7.
Declaration of Independence EXCERPT

On June 7, 1776, the Continental Congress met to hear Richard Henry Lee's resolution for independence. After much debate, a committee of five was appointed to draft a statement. The committee consisted of John Adams, Roger Sherman, Benjamin Franklin, Robert R. Livingston, and Thomas Jefferson, who wrote the first draft.

The final draft of the Declaration of Independence was adopted on July 4, 1776, and approved by the New York Convention on July 9. The document was later engrossed (copied into a large, clear hand) and signed by almost every member of Congress on August 2. John Hancock, President of the Congress, was the first to sign.

This is the introduction to the Declaration of Independence, the final version of which was penned by Thomas Jefferson. It was signed on July 4, 1776.

When in the Course of human events, it becomes necessary for one people to dissolve the political bands which have connected them with another, and to assume among the powers of the earth, the separate and equal station to which the Laws of Nature and of Nature's God entitle them, a decent respect to the opinions of mankind requires that they should declare the causes which impel them to the separation.

The text for this speech is the introduction and preamble of the Declaration. The remaining text includes the body and conclusion of the Declaration, which includes the list of the "long train of abuses and usurpations" made by King George III.

We hold these truths to be self-evident, that all men are created equal, that they are endowed by their Creator with certain unalienable Rights, that among these are Life, Liberty and the pursuit of Happiness. That to secure these rights, Governments are instituted among Men, deriving their just powers from the consent of the governed, That whenever any Form of Government becomes destructive of these ends, it is the Right of the People to alter or to abolish it, and to institute new Government, laying its foundation on such principles and organizing its powers in such form, as to them shall seem most likely to effect their Safety and Happiness. Prudence, indeed, will dictate that Governments long established should not be changed for light and transient causes; and accordingly all experience hath shewn, that mankind are more disposed to suffer, while evils are sufferable, than to right themselves by abolishing the forms to which they are accustomed. But when a long train of abuses and usurpations, pursuing invariably the same Object evinces a design to reduce them under absolute Despotism, it is their right, it is their duty, to throw off such Government, and to provide new Guards for their future security. Such has been the patient sufferance of these Colonies; and such is now the necessity which constrains them to alter their former Systems of Government. The history of the present King of Great Britain is a history of repeated injuries and usurpations, all having in direct object the establishment of an absolute Tyranny over these States. To prove this, let Facts be submitted to a candid world.

8.
Preamble to the Constitution of the United States of America

In 1787 the Federal Convention convened at Independence Hall in Philadelphia to revise the Articles of Confederation. After much debate in closed sessions, it became clear that it would be better to draft an entirely new frame of government. In closed sessions, the delegates debated and designed the new Constitution.

This short preamble to the entire work succinctly describes the purpose and guiding principles of the Constitution. The opening words, We the People, are enlarged and tie the Constitution to the Declaration. The Constitution was signed by the delegates on September 17, 1787.

This is the Preamble to the Constitution of the United States of America.

We the People of the United States, in Order to form a more perfect Union, establish Justice, insure domestic Tranquility, provide for the common defense, promote the general Welfare, and secure the Blessings of Liberty to ourselves and our Posterity, do ordain and establish this Constitution for the United States of America.

9.
1789 Abolition Speech

BY WILLIAM WILBERFORCE (1759–1833)

One of the most significant moments in the history of abolition is William Wilberforce's speech to the House of Commons in Parliament on May 12, 1789. After the four-hour speech, William Pitt, Prime Minister and close friend of Wilberforce, concluded:

> *"for the manner in which he had brought the subject before the House, not merely in regard to the masterly, forcible, and perspicuous mode of argument which he had pursued respecting it, but particularly for having chosen the only way in which it could be made obvious to the world, that they were warranted in every ground of fact and of reason, in coming to that vote, which he trusted would be the end of their proceeding."*

Although Parliament was moved by the speech, no action was taken. Year after year Wilberforce tirelessly kept the topic before the lawmakers. It would be another eighteen years before Parliament voted in favor of Wilberforce's Abolition of the Slave Trade Act. It became law on March 25, 1807.

An excerpt of an address given by William Wilberforce, May 12, 1789, to the House of Commons

The speech presented here is the introduction to Wilberforce's speech as presented in William Cobbett's *Parliamentary History of England*, 1811.

When I consider the magnitude of the subject which I am to bring before the House—a subject in which the interests, not of this country, nor of Europe alone, but of the whole world, and of posterity, are involved: and when I think, at the same time, on the weakness of the advocate who has undertaken this great cause—when these reflections press upon my mind, it is impossible for me not to feel both terrified and concerned at my own inadequacy to such a task.

But when I reflect, however, on the encouragement which I have had, through the whole course of a long and laborious examination of this question, and how much candour I have experienced, and how conviction has increased within my own mind, in proportion as I have advanced in my labours;—when I reflect, especially, that however averse any gentleman may now be, yet we shall all be of one opinion in the end;—when I turn myself to these thoughts, I take courage—I determine to forget all my other fears, and I march forward with a firmer step in the full assurance that my cause will bear me out, and that I shall be able to justify upon the clearest principles, every resolution in my hand, the avowed end of which is the total abolition of the slave trade.

I wish exceedingly, in the outset, to guard both myself and the House from entering into the subject with any sort of passion. It is not their passions I shall appeal to—I ask only for their cool and impartial reason; and I wish not to take them by surprise, but to deliberate, point by point, upon every part of this question. I mean not to accuse any one, but to take the shame upon myself, in common, indeed, with the whole parliament of Great Britain, for having suffered this horrid trade to be carried on under their authority. We are all guilty—we ought all to plead guilty, and not to exculpate ourselves by throwing the blame on others; and I therefore deprecate every kind of reflection against the various descriptions of people who are more immediately involved in this wretched business.

10.
What to the Slave Is the Fourth of July?

BY FREDERICK DOUGLASS (1818–1895)

Born a slave, Frederick Douglass became a well-known orator and writer. He learned to read at the age of twelve, and his new literacy led him to question slavery. He eventually escaped to New York at the age of twenty-one. He spent the rest of his life writing and speaking.

On July 5, 1852, Douglass was asked to speak in Rochester, New York, at an event commemorating the signing of the Declaration of Independence. The speech below is from the end of that speech. The entire text can be easily found online.

An excerpt from an address given by Frederick Douglass on July 5, 1852

Would you have me argue that man is entitled to liberty? that he is the rightful owner of his own body? You have already declared it. Must I argue the wrongfulness of slavery? Is that a question for Republicans? Is it to be settled by the rules of logic and argumentation, as a matter beset with great difficulty, involving a doubtful application of the principle of justice, hard to be understood? … There is not a man beneath the canopy of heaven that does not know that slavery is wrong for him.

Frederick Douglass's best-known work, *Narrative of the Life of Frederick Douglass, an American Slave*, was published in 1845.

At a time like this, scorching irony, not convincing argument, is needed. O! had I the ability, and could I reach the nation's ear, I would, to-day, pour out a fiery stream of biting ridicule, blasting reproach, withering sarcasm, and stern rebuke. For it is not light that is needed, but fire; it is not the gentle shower, but thunder. We need the storm, the whirlwind, and the earthquake. The feeling of the nation must be quickened; the conscience of the nation must be roused; the propriety of the nation must be startled; the hypocrisy of the nation must be exposed; and its crimes against God and man must be proclaimed and denounced.

What, to the American slave, is your 4th of July? I answer: a day that reveals to him, more than all other days in the year, the gross injustice and cruelty to which he is the constant victim. To him, your celebration is a sham; your boasted liberty, an unholy license; your national greatness, swelling vanity; your sounds of rejoicing are empty and heartless; your denunciations of tyrants, brass fronted impudence; your shouts of liberty and equality, hollow mockery; your prayers and hymns, your sermons and thanksgivings, with all your religious parade, and solemnity, are, to him, mere bombast, fraud, deception, impiety, and hypocrisy—a thin veil to cover up crimes which would disgrace a nation of savages. There is not a nation on the earth guilty of practices, more shocking and bloody, than are the people of these United States, at this very hour.

Go where you may, search where you will, roam through all the monarchies and despotisms of the old world, travel through South America, search out every abuse, and when you have found the last, lay your facts by the side of the everyday practices of this nation, and you will say with me, that, for revolting barbarity and shameless hypocrisy, America reigns without a rival.

11.
Opening Lines of *A Tale of Two Cities*

BY CHARLES DICKENS (1812–1870)

Charles Dickens is regarded as one of the greatest novelists of the Victorian era. A Tale of Two Cities *is set at the time of the French Revolution, involving characters from London and Paris. The book was published in weekly installments from April to November 1859 in Dickens's new magazine,* All the Year Round.

This is the opening paragraph of the novel *A Tale of Two Cities* by Charles Dickens.

It was the best of times, it was the worst of times, it was the age of wisdom, it was the age of foolishness, it was the epoch of belief, it was the epoch of incredulity, it was the season of Light, it was the season of Darkness, it was the spring of hope, it was the winter of despair, we had everything before us, we had nothing before us, we were all going direct to Heaven, we were all going direct the other way—in short, the period was so far like the present period, that some of its noisiest authorities insisted on its being received, for good or for evil, in the superlative degree of comparison only.

12.
The Gettysburg Address

BY ABRAHAM LINCOLN (1809–1865)

The Battle of Gettysburg was fought from July 1 to July 3 of 1863, leaving up to 51,000 soldiers from both sides missing, wounded, or killed. The dead had been hastily buried in makeshift graves along the battlefield. The Commonwealth of Pennsylvania purchased land to create a Soldiers' National Cemetery.

The cemetery was dedicated on November 19, 1863. Edward Everett, a famous orator, was invited to speak and President Lincoln was asked to formally "set apart these grounds to their sacred use by a few appropriate remarks." Everett spoke for two hours; Lincoln spoke for two minutes.

An address by Abraham Lincoln at the battlefield of Gettysburg, November 19, 1863

Four score and seven years ago our fathers brought forth on this continent, a new nation, conceived in Liberty, and dedicated to the proposition that all men are created equal.

There are five versions of the Gettysburg Address. The one reprinted here, known as the Bliss Copy, is the only one signed and dated by Lincoln. It is also the version inscribed on the Lincoln Memorial.

Now we are engaged in a great civil war, testing whether that nation, or any nation so conceived and so dedicated, can long endure. We are met on a great battle-field of that war. We have come to dedicate a portion of that field, as a final resting place for those who here gave their lives that that nation might live. It is altogether fitting and proper that we should do this.

But, in a larger sense, we can not dedicate—we can not consecrate—we can not hallow—this ground. The brave men, living and dead, who struggled here, have consecrated it, far above our poor power to add or detract. The world will little note, nor long remember what we say here, but it can never forget what they did here. It is for us the living, rather, to be dedicated here to the unfinished work which they who fought here have thus far so nobly advanced. It is rather for us to be here dedicated to the great task remaining before us—that from these honored dead we take increased devotion to that cause for which they gave the last full measure of devotion—that we here highly resolve that these dead shall not have died in vain—that this nation, under God, shall have a new birth of freedom—and that government of the people, by the people, for the people, shall not perish from the earth.

hallow: to make holy

Abraham Lincoln
November 19, 1863

13.
Address at a Gathering of Americans in London, July 4, 1872

BY MARK TWAIN (1835–1910)

One of the best known American writers is Mark Twain. Ernest Hemingway wrote, "All modern American literature comes from one book by Mark Twain called 'Huckleberry Finn.' There has been nothing as good since."

Samuel Langhorne Clemens was raised in Hannibal, Missouri. After apprenticing with a printer, Clemens became a riverboat pilot before turning to journalism where he adopted his pen name, Mark Twain. His pseudonym reflects his early life on the Mississippi River: "Mark Twain" means mark two *or* two fathoms, *the safe depth of water for a steamboat.*

In addition to writing, Twain was a popular speaker to audiences all over the world. This particular speech was excerpted from one that he gave to a group of Americans in London and illustrates Twain's friendly, funny, and satirical style.

From a speech by Mark Twain on July 4, 1872, given in London, England

I thank you for the compliment which has just been tendered me, and to show my appreciation of it I will not afflict you with many words.

It is pleasant to celebrate in this peaceful way, upon this old mother soil, the anniversary of an experiment which was born of war with this same land so long ago, and wrought out to a successful issue by the devotion of our ancestors. It has taken nearly a hundred years to bring the English and Americans into kindly and mutually appreciative relations, but I believe it has been accomplished at last.

... With a common origin, a common language, a common literature, a common religion, and common drinks, what is longer needful to the cementing of the two nations together in a permanent bond of brotherhood?

This is an age of progress, and ours is a progressive land. ...

We have a criminal jury system which is superior to any in the world; and its efficiency is only marred by the difficulty of finding twelve men every day who don't know anything and can't read. And I may observe that we have an insanity plea that would have saved Cain.

Cain, firstborn son of Adam and Eve, murdered his brother Abel.

I think I can say, and say with pride, that we have some legislatures that bring higher prices than any in the world.

I refer with effusion to our railway system, which consents to let us live, though it might do the opposite, being our owners. It only destroyed three thousand and seventy lives last year by collisions, and twenty-seven thousand two hundred and sixty by running over heedless and unnecessary people at crossings. The companies seriously regretted the killing of these thirty thousand people, and went so far as to pay for some of them—voluntarily, of course, for the meanest of us would not claim that we possess a court treacherous enough to enforce a law against a railway company. But, thank Heaven, the railway companies are generally disposed to do the right and kindly thing without compulsion ...

effusion: unrestrained outpouring of words with great emotion

But I must not stand here and brag all night. However, you won't mind a body bragging a little about his country on the Fourth of July. It is a fair and legitimate time to fly the eagle. I will say only one more word of brag—and a hopeful one. It is this. We have a form of government which gives each man a fair chance and no favor. With us no individual is born with a right to look down upon his neighbor and hold him in contempt. Let such of us as are not dukes find our consolation in that. And we may find hope for the future in the fact that as unhappy as is the condition of our political morality today, England has risen up out of a far fouler since the days when Charles I ennobled courtesans and all political place was a matter of bargain and sale.

In 1782, the bald **eagle** was chosen to appear on the Great Seal of the United States.

Charles I was king of England from 1625 to 1649. He was executed after being tried and found guilty of treason.

There is hope for us yet.

14.
Excerpts from "The Strenuous Life"

BY THEODORE ROOSEVELT (1859–1919)

Where does one start to introduce one of America's most colorful presidents? Theodore Roosevelt became a lifelong naturalist through self-study as a youth, explored the world with his father and family, excelled in boxing, led the courageous Rough Riders during the Spanish American War, worked as a cowboy and a deputy sheriff out west, published books on diverse subjects, and held a variety of public offices, including President of the United States from 1901–1909.

Roosevelt had stamina. While serving as a deputy sheriff, he captured three outlaws who had stolen his riverboat. To stay awake while guarding them for forty hours without sleep, he read Leo Tolstoy. During his time as police commissioner in New York, he walked the officer's beats at all hours to ensure that the police were on duty. As a captain of the Rough Riders, he and his men courageously took Kettle Hill in the face of heavy gunfire. Roosevelt was unstoppable.

Roosevelt spoke from experience as he gave this speech to a men's club during his term as governor of New York.

From an address by Theodore Roosevelt to the Hamilton Club in Chicago, Illinois, on April 10, 1899

… A life of slothful ease, a life of that peace which springs merely from lack either of desire or of power to strive after great things, is as little worthy of a nation as of an individual. I ask only that what every self-respecting American demands from himself and from his sons shall be demanded of the American nation as a whole. Who among you would teach your boys that ease, that peace, is to be the first consideration in their eyes—to be the ultimate goal after which they strive?

… You work yourselves, and you bring up your sons to work. If you are rich and are worth your salt, you will teach your sons that though they may have leisure, it is not to be spent in idleness; for wisely used leisure merely means that those who possess it, being free from the necessity of working for their livelihood, are all the more bound to carry on some kind of non-remunerative work in science, in letters, in art, in exploration, in historical research—work of the type we most need in this country, the successful carrying out of which reflects most honor upon the nation.

non-remunerative: not receiving a wage for one's work

We do not admire the man of timid peace. We admire the man who embodies victorious effort; the man who never wrongs his neighbor, who is prompt to help a friend, but who has those virile qualities necessary to win in the stern strife of actual life. It is hard to fail, but it is worse never to have tried to succeed. In this life we get nothing save by effort. Freedom from effort in the present merely means that there has been stored up effort in the past.

... A mere life of ease is not in the end a very satisfactory life, and, above all, it is a life which ultimately unfits those who follow it for serious work in the world.

In the last analysis a healthy state can exist only when the men and women who make it up lead clean, vigorous, healthy lives; when the children are so trained that they shall endeavor, not to shirk difficulties, but to overcome them; not to seek ease, but to know how to wrest triumph from toil and risk. The man must be glad to do a man's work, to dare and endure and to labor; to keep himself, and to keep those dependent upon him. The woman must be the housewife, the helpmeet of the homemaker, the wise and fearless mother of many healthy children. In one of Daudet's powerful and melancholy books he speaks of "the fear of maternity, the haunting terror of the young wife of the present day." When such words can be truthfully written of a nation, that nation is rotten to the heart's core. When men fear work or fear righteous war, when women fear motherhood, they tremble on the brink of doom; and well it is that they should vanish from the earth, where they are fit subjects for the scorn of all men and women who are themselves strong and brave and high-minded.

The quote is from a nineteenth-century novel, *The Immortal*, by Alphonse **Daudet**. In the book, an ambitious wife and spendthrift son treat the protagonist with contempt and neglect.

15. The King's Speech

BY KING GEORGE VI (1895–1952)

Albert Frederick Arthur George became king of England in 1936 after the abdication of his elder brother, Edward, earlier that year. The nation was not convinced that Albert, crowned George VI, would be a good king because he had a severe stutter, which people at the time equated with mental weakness.

Visit IEW.com/LDP-info for helpful links related to this speech.

Fortunately, the king's wife, Elizabeth, located a maverick Australian speech therapist named Lionel Logue who was able to help the king. After ten months of therapy, Logue had nearly cured the king of his difficulty.

The king's speech was put to the test on September 3, 1939, when George VI had to deliver a most important speech in his life: the announcement that England had declared war on Germany. He had to do it live. Standing at a lectern in a side room with the window open, King George gave the speech to a single person, Logue, as if he were just delivering it to a friend. It worked: The king's delivery was clear, calm, and dignified.

Nevertheless, the backstory of the king's speech should not outshine the speech itself that prepared a nation to face the deprivation and horrors of a second World War.

This is English King George VI's speech announcing the outbreak of war with Germany, delivered September 3, 1939.

George VI is pronounced George the Sixth.

In this grave hour, perhaps the most fateful in our history, I send to every household of my peoples, both at home and overseas, this message, spoken with the same depth of feeling for each one of you as if I were able to cross your threshold and speak to you myself.

For the second time in the lives of most of us, we are at war. Over and over again we have tried to find a peaceful way out of the differences between ourselves and those who are now our enemies. But it has been in vain. We have been forced into a conflict. For we are called, with our allies, to meet the challenge of a principle which, if it were to prevail, would be fatal to any civilised order in the world.

The king had served in the navy during World War I.

As of September 1, 1939, the Allies consisted of France, Poland, Great Britain, and soon the British Commonwealth (Canada, Australia, New Zealand, and South Africa). The Soviet Union and the United States joined the Allies in 1941.

It is the principle which permits a state, in the selfish pursuit of power, to disregard its treaties and its solemn pledges; which sanctions the use of force, or threat of force, against the sovereignty and independence of other states. Such a principle, stripped of all disguise, is surely the mere primitive doctrine that might is right; and if this principle were established throughout the world, the freedom of our own country and of the whole British Commonwealth of nations would be in danger. But far more than this—the peoples of the world would be kept in the bondage of fear, and all hopes of settled peace and of the security of justice and liberty among nations, would be ended.

This is the ultimate issue which confronts us. For the sake of all that we ourselves hold dear, and of the world's order and peace, it is unthinkable that we should refuse to meet the challenge.

It is to this high purpose that I now call my people at home and my peoples across the seas, who will make our cause their own.

I ask them to stand calm, firm and united in this time of trial. The task will be hard. There may be dark days ahead, and war can no longer be confined to the battlefield. But we can only do the right as we see the right, and reverently commit our cause to God. If one and all we keep resolutely faithful to it, ready for whatever service or sacrifice it may demand, then, with God's help, we shall prevail.

World War II was not confined to the battlefield. The bombing of London began in September 1940.

May He bless and keep us all.

16.
We Shall Fight on the Beaches

BY WINSTON CHURCHILL (1874–1965)

Winston Churchill became prime minister of Britain eight months after World War II broke out in Europe. Three days later in his first speech to the House of Commons, he announced, "I would say to the House, as I said to those who have joined this Government: 'I have nothing to offer but blood, toil, tears, and sweat.'"

If you would like to listen to Churchill give this speech, search for it on YouTube.

Throughout May 1940 the Germans had cut off the Allied forces. Belgium had capitulated. Soldiers had been hastily yet successfully evacuated from the perilous beaches of Dunkirk.

That was the context of this speech. A year later, American journalist H.R. Knickerbocker wrote that these words "deserve to be memorized by us all." And so we shall.

An excerpt of an address by Winston Churchill to the House of Commons on June 4, 1940

I have, myself, full confidence that if all do their duty, if nothing is neglected, and if the best arrangements are made, as they are being made, we shall prove ourselves once again able to defend our Island home, to ride out the storm of war, and to outlive the menace of tyranny, if necessary for years, if necessary alone. At any rate, that is what we are going to try to do. That is the resolve of His Majesty's Government—every man of them. That is the will of Parliament and the nation.

The British Empire and the French Republic, linked together in their cause and in their need, will defend to the death their native soil, aiding each other like good comrades to the utmost of their strength. Even though large tracts of Europe and many old and famous States have fallen or may fall into the grip of the Gestapo and all the odious apparatus of Nazi rule, we shall not flag or fail.

Gestapo: short for *Geheime Staatspolizel*, the Secret State Police. This organization did not have any civil restraints and was ruthless in the elimination of any opposition against the Nazis.

We shall go on to the end, we shall fight in France, we shall fight on the seas and oceans, we shall fight with growing confidence and growing strength in the air, we shall defend our Island, whatever the cost may be, we shall fight on the beaches, we shall fight on the landing grounds, we shall fight in the fields and in the streets, we shall fight in the hills; we shall never surrender, and even if, which I do not for a moment believe, this Island or a large part of it were subjugated and starving, then our Empire beyond the seas, armed and guarded by the British Fleet, would carry on the struggle, until, in God's good time, the New World, with all its power and might, steps forth to the rescue and the liberation of the old.

17.
For We Let Our Young Men and Women Go Out Unarmed

BY DOROTHY SAYERS (1893–1957)

Although Dorothy Sayers is best known for her mystery novels, she also wrote poetry, translated several ancient works of literature, and wrote many essays.

In 1947 Sayers read her essay, "The Lost Tools of Learning," at a Vacation Course in Education at Oxford. In the essay, Sayers mused that despite the additional years that modern students spend in school, the ability to think independently and argue a position are sorely lacking. She explored the syllabus of a Medieval education, the Trivium and Quadrivium, and how they could apply to education today.

An excerpt of a paper given by Dorothy Sayers at Oxford University in 1947

For we let our young men and women go out unarmed, in a day when armor was never so necessary. By teaching them all to read, we have left them at the mercy of the printed word. By the invention of the film and the radio, we have made certain that no aversion to reading shall secure them from the incessant battery of words, words, words. They do not know what the words mean; they do not know how to ward them off or blunt their edge or fling them back; they are a prey to words in their emotions instead of being the masters of them in their intellects. We who were scandalized in 1940 when men were sent to fight armored tanks with rifles, are not scandalized when young men and women are sent into the world to fight massed propaganda with a smattering of "subjects"; and when whole classes and whole nations become hypnotized by the arts of the spell binder, we have the impudence to be astonished. We dole out lip-service to the importance of education—lip-service and, just occasionally, a little grant of money; we postpone the school-leaving age, and plan to build bigger and better schools; the teachers slave conscientiously in and out of school hours; and yet, as I believe, all this devoted effort is largely frustrated, because we have lost the tools of learning, and in their absence can only make a botched and piecemeal job of it.

propaganda: ideas and statements, often false or exaggerated, that are spread in order to help a cause or political leader

18.
Anyway

BY MOTHER TERESA (1910–1997)

Agnes Gonxha Bojaxhiu took the name Sister Teresa when she joined the Sisters of Loreto in Calcutta, India, where she taught in the order's school for seventeen years. Later, she was called to devote herself to caring for the sick and poor, founding the Missionaries of Charity and becoming Mother Teresa.

Adopting Indian citizenship, Mother Teresa opened numerous centers to serve the dying, lepers, the blind, the aged, and the disabled. In 1979 she was awarded the Nobel Peace Prize "for work undertaken in the struggle to overcome poverty and distress, which also constitutes a threat to peace."

It is reported that this poem was written on the wall of one of her homes for children in Calcutta, and the poem has been attributed to her. It is based on "The Paradoxical Commandments" by Kent Keith.

This is often titled "Anyway" and is attributed to Mother Teresa, who lived from 1910 to 1997.

People are often unreasonable, irrational, and self-centered.
  Forgive them anyway.

If you are kind, people may accuse you of selfish, ulterior motives.
  Be kind anyway.

If you are successful, you will win some unfaithful friends
  and some genuine enemies.
  Succeed anyway.

If you are honest and sincere people may deceive you.
  Be honest and sincere anyway.

What you spend years creating, others could destroy overnight.
  Create anyway.

If you find serenity and happiness, some may be jealous.
  Be happy anyway.

The good you do today will often be forgotten.
  Do good anyway.

Give the best you have, and it will never be enough.
  Give your best anyway.

In the final analysis, it is between you and God.
  It was never between you and them anyway.

The "Paradoxical Commandments" by Keith does not include this last stanza.

19.
Brandenburg Gate Speech

BY RONALD REAGAN (1911–2004)

Visit IEW.com/LDP-info for a link to watch the entire speech.

After World War II, Germany was occupied by the Allied powers: the United States, Great Britain, France, and the Soviet Union. Germany's capital was similarly divided. Eventually the three zones occupied by free countries united to become West Germany while the section under the control of the communist Soviet Union became East Germany.

Set up as a capitalist society and with the help and support of its occupiers, West Germany flourished. East Germany suffered under the influence of the Soviet Union. Its economy was hindered and its people's freedoms curtailed.

As a result, many people living in East Germany fled to West Germany. Although many were stopped at the border, millions made it across the border. In the middle of the night in August of 1961, the Berlin Wall was constructed, complete with barbed wire. Even the telephone wires connecting the two sides of the city were cut. The wall symbolized the division of East and West during the Cold War, a term first used by George Orwell in an article predicting the future nuclear stalemate.

The eighteenth-century Brandenburg Gate became a symbol of freedom. John F. Kennedy delivered his famous "Ich Bin ein Berliner" speech at the site. Although Reagan addressed Germans on both sides of the wall, police kept its citizens far enough back that it is unlikely that they could hear.

In 1989 a series of political changes led to the announcement on November 9, 1989, that East German citizens could visit West Germany and West Berlin. Elated, both sides began to chip away at the wall until in 1992 nothing was left.

President Ronald Reagan, address from the Brandenburg Gate at the Berlin Wall, June 12, 1987, excerpt

Behind me stands a wall that encircles the free sectors of this city, part of a vast system of barriers that divides the entire continent of Europe. From the Baltic, south, those barriers cut across Germany in a gash of barbed wire, concrete, dog runs, and guardtowers. …

Where four decades ago there was rubble, today in West Berlin there is the greatest industrial output of any city in Germany: busy office blocks, fine homes and apartments, proud avenues, and the spreading lawns of parkland. Where a city's culture seemed to have been destroyed, today there are two great universities, orchestras and an opera, countless theaters, and museums. Where there was want, today there's abundance—food, clothing, automobiles. … From devastation, from utter ruin, you Berliners have, in freedom, rebuilt a city that once again ranks as one of the greatest on Earth. …

In the 1950s, Khrushchev predicted: "We will bury you." But in the West today, we see a free world that has achieved a level of prosperity and well-being unprecedented in all human history. In the Communist world, we see failure, technological backwardness, declining standards of health, even want of the most basic kind—too little food. Even today, the Soviet Union still cannot feed itself. After these four decades, then, there stands before the entire world one great and inescapable conclusion: Freedom leads to prosperity. Freedom replaces the ancient hatreds among the nations with comity and peace. Freedom is the victor. …

Nikita **Khrushchev** served as premier of the Soviet Union from 1958 to 1964. The full quote was "Whether you like it or not, we are on the right side of history. We will bury you." He was referring to what he considered to be the inevitable progression of societies. When capitalism died, communism would be there to bury it.

And now the Soviets themselves may, in a limited way, be coming to understand the importance of freedom. We hear much from Moscow about a new policy of reform and openness. Some political prisoners have been released. Certain foreign news broadcasts are no longer being jammed. Some economic enterprises have been permitted to operate with greater freedom from state control. Are these the beginnings of profound changes in the Soviet state? Or are they token gestures, intended to raise false hopes in the West, or to strengthen the Soviet system without changing it? We welcome change and openness; for we believe that freedom and security go together, that the advance of human liberty can only strengthen the cause of world peace.

There is one sign the Soviets can make that would be unmistakable, that would advance dramatically the cause of freedom and peace. General Secretary Gorbachev, if you seek peace, if you seek prosperity for the Soviet Union and Eastern Europe, if you seek liberalization: Come here to this gate! Mr. Gorbachev, open this gate! Mr. Gorbachev, tear down this wall!

20.
Freedom from Fear Speech

BY AUNG SAN SUU KYI (1945–)

A link to the entire speech can be found at IEW.com/LDP-info.

Aung San Suu Kyi's father, Aung San, was responsible for negotiating the independence of Burma (modern-day Myanmar) from Britain in 1947. Unfortunately, political rivals assassinated Aung San within that same year.

After years of socialism, the long-time military leader of Burma stepped down. After a violent uprising on August 8, 1988, Suu Kyi addressed a huge crowd at the capital, calling for a democratic government. She founded the National League for Democracy, but was placed under house arrest by the military rulers in 1989.

Suu Kyi remained under house arrest for fifteen of the next twenty-one years. She spent her time studying, writing, and speaking. She was awarded the Nobel Peace Prize in 1991, but since she was still under house arrest, her son accepted the award in her place. She finally had the opportunity to accept the prize in person in 2012.

An excerpt from an address by Aung San Suu Kyi, 1990

The wellspring of courage and endurance in the face of unbridled power is generally a firm belief in the sanctity of ethical principles combined with a historical sense that despite all setbacks the condition of man is set on an ultimate course for both spiritual and material advancement. It is his capacity for self-improvement and self-redemption which most distinguishes man from the mere brute. At the root of human responsibility is the concept of perfection, the urge to achieve it, the intelligence to find a path towards it, and the will to follow that path if not to the end at least the distance needed to rise above individual limitations and environmental impediments. It is man's vision of a world fit for rational, civilized humanity which leads him to dare and to suffer to build societies free from want and fear. Concepts such as truth, justice and compassion cannot be dismissed as trite when these are often the only bulwarks which stand against ruthless power.

Speech Suggestions

Most of the speeches listed below are quite long. Therefore, we recommend that students choose one to three paragraphs to memorize. Teachers or parents may wish to read the entire speech to help students select paragraphs which contain the most compelling, eloquent, or inspiring language.

St. Francis of Assisi, "Sermon to the Birds," circa 1220

James Madison, The Bill of Rights (first ten amendments to the U.S. Constitution), ratified December 15, 1791

Abraham Lincoln, "House Divided" speech given after his nomination to candidacy for the U.S. Senate, June 16, 1858: "I believe this government cannot endure, permanently half slave and half free."

Abraham Lincoln, Second Inaugural Address, March 4, 1865: "With malice toward none, with charity for all ..."

George Graham Vest, "A Tribute to the Dog," closing argument on behalf of the plaintiff in *Burden v. Hornsby*, September 23, 1870

Booker T. Washington, "The American Standard" speech to the Harvard Alumni June 24, 1896, upon receiving an honorary Master of Arts degree: "Why you have called me from the Black Belt of the South ..."

Woodrow Wilson, "Peace without Victory" speech before the U.S. Senate during World War I, January 22, 1917

Mohandas Gandhi, "Non-Cooperation" speech to the Indian National Congress, August 12, 1920: "There shall be no cooperation between injustice and justice ..."

Lady Astor, "Women in Politics" speech April 9, 1922: "I can conceive of nothing worse than a man-governed world except a woman-governed world ..."

Franklin D. Roosevelt, First Inaugural Address, March 4, 1933: "The only thing we have to fear is fear itself ..."

Franklin D. Roosevelt, Second Inaugural Address, January 20, 1937: "Government is competent when ..."

Winston Churchill, "Blood, Sweat, Toil and Tears" speech to the British House of Commons, May 13, 1940

Winston Churchill, "Their Finest Hour" speech to the British House of Commons, June 18, 1940

Franklin D. Roosevelt, "The Four Freedoms" speech (State of the Union address), January 6, 1941: "In the future days … we look forward to a world founded upon four essential human freedoms."

Pope Pius XII, Easter Message from the Vatican, April 13, 1941: "In the lamentable spectacle of human conflict which we are now witnessing …"

Dwight D. Eisenhower, "The Great Crusade" statement to soldiers, sailors, and airmen of the Allied Expeditionary Force, June 5, 1944, the day before the D-Day invasion

Martin Luther King, Jr., "I Have a Dream" speech delivered August 28, 1963: "I have a dream that one day this nation will rise up and live out the true meaning of its creed."

Lyndon B. Johnson, "The American Promise" speech to a joint session of Congress proposing the Voting Rights Act, following the violence during the Civil Rights March in Selma, Alabama, March 15, 1965: "Our mission is at once the oldest …"

Pope Paul VI, "No More War" address to the United Nations, October 4, 1965

Soliloquy Suggestions from the Plays of William Shakespeare

Shylock's soliloquy in *The Merchant of Venice*, Act III, Scene i
"If you prick us do we not bleed?"

Brutus's soliloquy in *Julius Caesar*, Act III, Scene ii
"Romans, countrymen, and lovers! Hear me for my cause ..."

Rosalind's fiery soliloquy in *As You Like It*, Act III, Scene v
"And why I pray you?"

Jacque's oration, *As You Like It*, Act II, Scene vii
"All the world's a stage ..."

Friar Lawrence in response to Romeo's banishment behavior, *Romeo and Juliet*, Act III, Scene iii
"Hold thy desperate hand. Art thou a man? Thy form cries out thou art ..."

Juliet before taking the sleeping potion, *Romeo and Juliet*, Act IV, Scene iii
"Farewell! God knows when we shall meet again ..."

Juliet on balcony, *Romeo and Juliet*, Act II, Scene ii
"O Romeo, Romeo! Wherefore art thou Romeo?"

Romeo on balcony, *Romeo and Juliet*, Act II, Scene ii
"But soft, what light through yonder window breaks?"

Romeo before his suicide, *Romeo and Juliet*, Act V, Scene iii
"In faith, I will. Let me peruse this face: Mercutio's kinsman, noble Count Paris ..."

Amien's song, *As You Like It*, Act II, Scene vii
"Blow, blow thou winter wind ..."

Richard's opening soliloquy, *Richard III*
"Now is the winter of our discontent ..."

Hamlet's soliloquy, *Hamlet*, Act III, Scene i
"To be or not to be ..."

Macbeth in *Macbeth*, Act V, Scene v
"Tomorrow, and tomorrow, and tomorrow ..."

Macbeth in *Macbeth*, Act II, Scene i
"Is this a dagger which I see before me?"

CERTIFICATE OF COMPLETION

This certifies that

____

has successfully completed the memorization and presentation requirements for

LEVEL FIVE OF

Linguistic Development through Poetry Memorization

____________________ DATE

Listen. Speak. Read. Write. Think!

____________________ SUPERVISOR

Appendix 1
BIOGRAPHIES

A

Growing up in New England surrounded by her father's peers—among whom were Hawthorne, Emerson, and Thoreau—the prodigious author **Louisa May Alcott** (1832–1888) wrote books, plays, poems, and short stories. Her outstanding novels wove charming tales about families like her own. Her greatest books, *Little Women*, *Little Men*, and *Jo's Boys*, are considered classics of American Literature.

› *A Song from the Suds, page 106*

Dave Arns is achieving literary notoriety with his amusing thesaurusoetry. His recent collection *Mother Goose, Ph.D.*, was imagineered in 1987. Thesaurusoetry challenges the reader to translate intellectual, technical verbiage into what are actually familiar rhymes that have been cleverly obscured through the use of synonyms.

› *Scintillate, Scintillate, Globule Vivific, page 68*

B

George Linnaeus Banks (1821–1881) was a British journalist, editor, poet, and playwright. His wife, Isabella, was also a published poet and novelist. His father was a horticulturalist, which may explain his middle name.

› *What I Live For, page 69*

Hilaire Belloc (1870–1953) was a prolific writer of novels, poetry, and essays; a captivating speaker, he toured the United States. Belloc, usually embroiled in controversy, held a seat in Parliament. Along with his contemporary G.K. Chesterton, he espoused moral and economic theories that denounced Socialism and favored both small farmers and businesses.

› *The Vulture, page 10*
› *The Yak, page 13*
› *Rebecca, Who Slammed Doors for Fun and Perished Miserably, page 35*
› *Matilda, Who Told Lies, and Was Burned to Death, page 67*

William John Bennett was born in 1943 of a middle-class family. He grew up in Brooklyn, New York, and became a scholar and a teacher, stating that heroic American men such as Abraham Lincoln and Roy Campanella were his role models.

› *The Ingenious Little Old Man, page 14*

William Blake (1757–1827) was artistically gifted in writing, engraving, drawing, and painting. He was born and raised in England, and he reported that his mystical writings and spiritual works of art followed from the visions he received of the angels and saints. "The Tiger" is his most famous poem.

› *The Tiger, page 94*

Most of her publications were serious: British writer and poet **Beatrice Curtis Brown** (1901–1974) authored at least eleven books including a history of England and biographies of inspirational British women. But she could write very funny poems, too, such as "Jonathan Bing."

› *Jonathan Bing, page 17*

Intriguingly reputed as a "haughty and aristocratic genius," **George Gordon, Lord Byron** (1788–1824) is one of the most important English poets. He wrote tender love ballads like "She Walks in Beauty" as well as exciting battle poems such as "The Eve of Waterloo." He died from a fever when he was only thirty-six after being caught in the rain while horseback riding.

› *The Destruction of Sennacherib, page 79*

C

Sir Lewis Carroll's real name was Charles Dodgson. Having been homeschooled in England by his mother until the age of twelve, he wrote essays, short stories, books, and poetry from his earliest adolescence and created such characters as the Mock Turtle, the Cheshire Cat, and the Jabberwocky. The heroine of his phenomenally successful book *Alice's Adventures in Wonderland* seems to have been named after a favorite sister. He lived from 1832 to 1898.

› *How Doth the Little Crocodile, page 33*
› *Jabberwocky, page 40*

Guy Wetmore Carryl (1873–1904) was an American humorist. He authored over a dozen books including novels and poetry collections. Some critics have called him flippant. The parody "The Embarrassing Episode of Little Miss Muffet" is from a larger work, *Fables for the Frivolous.*

› *The Embarrassing Episode of Little Miss Muffet, page 93*
› *The Sycophantic Fox and the Gullible Raven, page 105*

Authors George Bernard Shaw, C.S. Lewis, and T.S. Eliot were deeply influenced by **G.K. Chesterton** (1874–1936). He has been called one of the greatest writers and apologists for the Christian faith in the twentieth century. He authored some one hundred books including the classics *The Everlasting Man* and *Orthodoxy*, and also wrote poetry, the Father Brown mystery series, and humor. Chesterton observed, "A good novel tells us the truth about its hero, but a bad novel tells us the truth about its author."

› *The Hunting of the Dragon, page 112*

Another English writer, **Samuel Taylor Coleridge** (1772–1834), co-authored a volume of verse with William Wordsworth. He originated the phrases, "water, water everywhere but not a drop to drink" and "an albatross around one's neck." He is best known for his poem "The Rime of the Ancient Mariner."

› *Epigram, page 103*

D

Walter de la Mare (1873–1956) is remembered for his children's literature. He first began writing seriously while working as an accountant, jotting down poems during free moments. "The Listeners" is probably his most famous poem.

› *Some One, page 37*

In this century, **John Dryden** (1631–1700) is recognized for translations of works by Virgil; he is also known for his poetry having to do with the politics of England during the Tudor monarchies and following. However, while he was alive, he achieved fame through his plays. "Grand Chorus" is the final verse of a larger work entitled "A Song for St. Cecilia's Day."

› *Grand Chorus, page 110*

Paul Laurence Dunbar (1872–1906) was the son of two freed African American slaves; because they passed on their oral tradition, he was able to champion black Americans by way of his songs, fiction, and poetry. He has been called the Poet Laureate of the Negro Race, and during his lifetime Frederick Douglass, W.E.B. Du Bois, and Booker T. Washington praised his work. Other outstanding poems include "We Wear the Mask" and "Sympathy." In the latter, Dunbar penned the poignant words, "I know why the caged bird sings."

› *Conscience and Remorse, page 50*

E

Max Ehrmann (1872–1945) became a successful lawyer; however, he chose to write full time when he was forty. The prose-poem "Desiderata" first gained him literary acclaim; in addition to poetry he published books, essays, and pamphlets.

› *Desiderata, page 108*

George Eliot was the pseudonym of British author Mary Ann Evans (1819–80), who wrote the novels *The Mill on the Floss* and *Silas Marner*. She used a pen name in order to guard her privacy and ensure that her work was taken seriously. Eliot is compared to Jane Austen because she attempted to expose the hypocrisy of the social class of English country squires.

› *The Choir Invisible, page 98*

Sister Mary Eulalia, RSM, was a Catholic nun of the Sisters of Mercy of the Americas. Their mission is to serve the poor and needy as teachers, nurses, and in various community outreach programs. Sister Eulalia died in 1984.

› *Courage, page 70*

F

James T. Fields (1817–81) was an esteemed American publisher. He helped to bring major authors such as Dickens, Tennyson, Hawthorne, and Harriet Beecher Stowe to the public. His humorous poem "The Owl Critic" is also an enjoyable piece.

› *Ballad of the Tempest, page 45*

Robert Frost, dubbed America's unofficial poet laureate, was the first poet to read at a presidential inauguration, reciting his poem "The Gift Outright" at the swearing in of John F. Kennedy. He achieved critical acclaim in his own lifetime (1874–1963) and received the Pulitzer Prize for Poetry four times. Frost typically combined solitary themes with images of nature, as in two of his beloved poems "Stopping by Woods on a Snowy Evening" and "The Road Not Taken."

› *Stopping by Woods on a Snowy Evening, page 51*
› *The Road Not Taken, page 65*

As a young schoolteacher in England, **Rose Fyleman** (1877–1957) supplied her students with the original poetry she enjoyed generating. Eventually, over sixty volumes of her poetry, fiction, and plays for children were published. Fyleman studied to become an opera singer and also gave voice lessons, which explains her charming enthusiasm for music!

› *Singing Time, page 12*

H

Oliver Herford (1863–1935) was a stand-up comedian who also wrote children's poetry and illustrated and published cartoons; he came from a large family of authors and artists. His friends nicknamed him "Peter Pan" because of his innocent, quick humor. Herford described a pest as "a man who can talk like an encyclopedia and does." Other funny poems for the young at heart include his "The Chimpanzee" and "The Hippopotamus."

› *Metaphysics, page 95*
› *The Hen, page 107*

Amazingly, nineteenth century American essayist, poet, novelist, and medical journalist **Oliver Wendell Holmes** achieved his literary prowess while chairing the Dartmouth and Harvard Anatomy and Physiology Departments from 1838 to 1892. His prose and poetry are celebrated as witty, brilliant, youthful, and original. He also wrote "Old Ironsides" and "The Last Leaf."

› *The Height of the Ridiculous, page 41*
› *God Save the Flag, page 104*

As a girl, **Mary Howitt** (1799–1888) was tutored at her home in England. She grew up in a loving family as evidenced by her poem entitled "The Clock is on the Stroke of Six," in which children eagerly await their father's arrival home from work. Howitt translated some of the stories of Hans Christian Andersen into German and co-authored several histories with her husband, William.

› *The Spider and the Fly, page 42*

James Henry Leigh Hunt (1784–1859) was a British poet, drama critic, editor, and essayist whose radical political views not only led him into camaraderie with other poet/reformers such as Percy Bysshe Shelley and Lord Byron, but also into prison. He penned the charming "Jenny Kissed Me," and his other well-loved poem is "Abou Ben Adhem," which according to research seems to have been memorized by countless grade school children prior to the 1960s. Enjoy!

› *The Glove and the Lions, page 49*

K

"Trees" is **Alfred Joyce Kilmer**'s most famous poem. This American writer died in battle in France in 1918.

› *Trees, page 44*

Benjamin Franklin King (1857–94) is a lesser-known American poet and journalist. He was born in Michigan, raised a family in Chicago, and gave public readings. A collection of his children's poetry can be found in *Ben King's Verse*, 1894.

› *The Pessimist, page 74*

L

Edward Lear (1812–88) wrote limericks, you say? Nonsense!

› *There Was an Old Person Whose Habits, page 16*

› *A Young Lady Named Bright, page 63*

American author **William Ellery Leonard** (1876–1944) wrote many books, an autobiography, and several poetry collections. His translations of the epic poems *Beowulf* and *De Rerum Natura* (*On the Nature of Things*) by Roman philosopher Lucretius (50 B.C.) are considered his noteworthy achievements.

› *The Swan and the Goose, page 25*

The poetry of **Henry Wadsworth Longfellow** (1807–1882) enjoyed large readership in its day because of its romantic treatment of simple stories, for example, "The Village Blacksmith." He has been called the most popular American poet of the nineteenth century. Other celebrated works are "The Song of Hiawatha" and "The Midnight Ride of Paul Revere."

› *A Psalm of Life, page 64*

› *The Village Blacksmith, page 80*

M

When he was a boy, **John Masefield** went to sea. After he published two volumes about his watery adventures, he was nicknamed "Poet of the Sea." In addition to poems like "Sea Fever," he is also remembered for his fine plays and novels. Masefield was Poet Laureate of England from 1930 until his death in 1967.

› *Sea Fever, page 47*

Sitting on the back step of an ambulance, anguished Canadian doctor **John McCrae** (1872–1918) put down the words of the haunting poem "In Flanders Fields" after treating injured soldiers in Belgium during World War I. The wild poppies to which he referred blossomed on the grisly battlefields of the Western Front where no other plants would grow.

› *In Flanders Fields, page 102*

Some students of literature may find the life and works of **Hughes Mearns** (1875–1965) quite interesting. This influential American was the first educator to teach creative writing as a subject in its own right, the goal of which was to foster the emotional, spiritual, and intellectual growth of students. He penned his most famous piece "The Little Man Who Wasn't There," also known as "Antigonish," when he was twenty-four.

› *The Little Man Who Wasn't There, page 9*

One of his biographers pronounced **Herman Melville** (1819–91) the greatest imaginative writer America had produced. *Moby Dick* was his masterful whale tale.

› *The Maldive Shark, page 100*

Another American author **George P. Morris** (1802–64) is primarily remembered as a poet. He also edited a magazine and composed hymns, such as the prayerful "Searcher of Hearts, from Mine Erase."

› *Woodman, Spare that Tree! page 109*

N

Ogden Nash (1902–71) was internationally famous as an author of extremely clever and amusing poems. Nash utilized the element of surprise, absurd plays on words, and newly invented words; persons of all ages have enjoyed his work. Despite all the silliness, however, Nash had a gift for touching upon the truths of the human experience.

› *Celery, page 8*

R

William Brighty Rands (1823–82) contributed to English periodicals and published several volumes of children's poetry. "Great, Wide, Beautiful, Wonderful World" is another of his well-known poems.

› *Godfrey Gordon Gustavus Gore, page 19*

Grantland Rice (1880–1954) is commonly acknowledged as the greatest American sportswriter. He coined the phrase "It's not whether you win or lose, it's how you play the game" and nicknamed the "Four Horsemen of Notre Dame." He authored many books about sports. Often inserting his own poetry into his columns, Rice wrote "Game Called" upon the death of Babe Ruth.

› *Casey's Revenge, page 82*

Billy Rose (1899–1966) was a famous American showman. He sang, composed, and produced lavish musical plays. Rose married the Vaudeville comedienne Fanny Brice and composed the song "It's Only a Paper Moon."

› *The Unknown Soldier, page 73*

Her father, Gabbriele Rossetti, and brother Dante, also poets, were influential in **Christina Rossetti**'s success as a writer. Because she was a devout Christian, many of her poems are religious in nature. The poem "My Gift" is a stanza from "A Christmas Carol" which was set to music. She lived from 1830 to 1894 in London.

› *My Gift, page 20*
› *Who Has Seen the Wind? page 23*

S

Internationally acclaimed author-poet **Carl Sandburg** (1878–1967) was the son of Swedish immigrants who settled in Illinois. After a college professor encouraged Sandburg to write, he became a journalist. He was awarded the Pulitzer Prize for his four-volume biography *Abraham Lincoln: The War Years*; he won a second time for *Complete Poems*. Sandburg is beloved for his free verse and down-to-earth words about the geography and the experience of the common people of America.

› *Fog, page 36*

The author **Sir Walter Scott** (1771–1832) was a famous son of Edinburgh, Scotland, where he grew up learning the ancient stories of his country. He employed this oral tradition in his lengthy narrative poems such as "The Lady of the Lake" and in his novels such as *Ivanhoe*.

› *Lochinvar, page 96*

William Shakespeare is the most widely studied British writer of all time. He lived from 1564 to 1616 during the reign of Queen Elizabeth I. "The Bard" penned many poems, and his matchless plays include comedies, dark histories like *Richard III*, and timeless tragedies such as *Hamlet* and *Romeo and Juliet*.

› *The Quality of Mercy from The Merchant of Venice, page 101*

The famous Southern poet **Edward Rowland Sill**, better known by the pseudonym Sidney Lanier (1842–1881), grew up in Georgia. Although he was captured and confined for five months in a squalid Union Army prison, he went on to lecture at a university, author a fiction series for boys, and compose many remarkably optimistic, faith-filled poems such as "The Symphony" and his masterpiece, "Sunrise." Coming from a long line of gifted musicians, Lanier was acclaimed as a musical genius on the flute. Unfortunately, he died at the age of thirty-nine. In a letter he wrote, "A thousand songs are singing in my heart that will certainly kill me if I do not utter them soon."

› *The Fool's Prayer, page 75*

Robert Louis Stevenson was a Scottish poet, novelist, and essayist who lived from 1850 to 1894. This master storyteller initially gained fame with the swashbuckling adventure *Treasure Island*. His novel of mystery and murder, *The Strange Case of Dr. Jekyll and Mr. Hyde*, has been adapted for the screen twenty times. However, he is equally well known for his 1885 volume of poetry for children, *A Child's Garden of Verses*.

› *My Shadow, page 15*
› *Whole Duty of Children, page 18*
› *The Swing, page 29*
› *At the Seaside, page 34*

T

Literary critics throughout the years have both lauded the works of **Alfred, Lord Tennyson** (1809–92) as philosophically important and decried them as sentimental and self-involved. Nevertheless, he is currently regarded as one of the great British poets. His major achievements are "In Memoriam," "The Charge of the Light Brigade," and "Ulysses."

› *The Eagle, page 24*
› *The Charge of the Light Brigade, page 46*

The American author **Ernest L. Thayer** (1863–1940) was a quiet, retiring man who wrote humor columns in the *San Francisco Examiner* for his Harvard classmate William Randolph Hearst. After he created "Casey at the Bat," he never submitted any other poem for publication.

› *Casey at the Bat, page 76*

U

New York-born **Louis Untermeyer** (1885–1977) is appreciated for the writing of his own poetry as well as for the gathering of other poets' verses into valuable compendia such as *This Singing World* and *Selected Poems and Parodies.*

› *Shoes, page 48*

W

"The hand that rocks the cradle is the hand that rules the world," wrote **William Ross Wallace** (1819–81) in praise of motherhood. Although he is not much remembered today, his patriotic poems such as "The Liberty Bell" and "Last Words of Washington" were inspirational to Union soldiers during the Civil War.

› *The Hand That Rocks the Cradle Is the Hand That Rules the World, page 99*

Myra Brooks Welch's masterpiece was "The Touch of the Master's Hand." She is called "The Poet with the Singing Soul." Welch came from a family of musicians and was an organist until she became challenged by severe arthritis. No longer able to play, she typed out her poetry with the eraser ends of two pencils, one in each hand.

› *The Touch of the Master's Hand, page 72*

Carolyn Wells (1869–1942) was an American poet and anthologist. *In Such Nonsense: An Anthology*, she penned especially comical, satirical poetry.

› *An Overworked Elocutionist, page 111*

Although **Walt Whitman**'s (1819–92) poems received mixed criticism by his contemporaries, he is an honored American writer. Primarily self-taught, he became a printer's apprentice at age eleven. By age sixteen he was helping to support his family as an editor and freelance writer. The poem "Leaves of Grass" was his life's work.

› *O Captain! My Captain! page 66*
› *When I Heard the Learn'd Astronomer, page 81*

Mary Fabyan Windeatt's biographies of saints such as Benedict, Thomas Aquinas, and Catherine of Siena are currently best sellers in the juvenile nonfiction genre. She lived from 1811 to 1873 in England. Curiously, historians have more to report about her colorful father and her husband than about the genuinely talented member of the family—writer Mary.

› *Project, page 52*

William Wise (1923–), popular with children as well as fun-loving adults, was an American author of fiction and nonfiction. He authored rhyming picture books for the very young, whimsical poetry, and historical novels.

› *After the Party, page 11*

During his day American songwriter **Henry Clay Work** (1832–84) was equally as popular as fellow Civil War composer Stephen Foster. Work wrote some one hundred songs. "Grandfather's Clock" sold almost one million copies when the sheet music was published.

› *Grandfather's Clock, page 71*

Y

Winner of the 1923 Nobel Prize for Literature, **William Butler Yeats** (1819–1939) is recognized as one of the greatest poets of the twentieth century. Irish born, he drew inspiration from the folklore of his country. He also wrote plays and was a senator and cultural leader. Two of his other famous fantasy-like poems are "The Everlasting Voices" and "When You Are Old."

› *He Wishes for the Cloths of Heaven, page 78*

Appendix 2
BIBLIOGRAPHY

Bennett, William J., ed. *The Book of Virtues—A Treasury of Great Moral Stories*. New York: Simon & Schuster, 1993.

Bennett, William J., ed. *The Moral Compass—Stories for a Life's Journey*. New York: Simon & Schuster, 1995.

Berquist, Laura M. *The Harp and Laurel Wreath*. San Francisco: Ignatius Press, 1999.

Blishen, Edward, ed. *Oxford Book of Poetry for Children*. New York: Peter Bedrick Books, 1984.

Bloom, Harold, ed. *Stories and Poems for Extremely Intelligent Children of All Ages*. New York: Scribner, 2001.

Carman, Bliss, ed. *The Oxford Book of American Verse*. U. S.: Oxford University Press, 1927.

Copeland, Lewis and Lawrence W. Lamm, eds. *The World's Great Speeches*. New York: Dover Publications, 1973.

The Editorial Board of the University Society, eds. *The Home University Bookshelf Vol. V Famous Stories and Verse*. New York: The University Society, 1927.

Felleman, Hazel, ed. *The Best-Loved Poems of the American People*. New York: Doubleday, 1936.

Ferris, Helen, ed. *Favorite Poems Old and New*. New York: Doubleday & Company, Inc., 1957.

Hohn, Max T., ed. *Stories in Verse*. Indiana: The Bobbs-Merrill Company, Inc., 1978.

Lear, Edward. *A Book of Nonsense*. New York: Alfred A. Knopf, Inc., 1992.

A Treasury of the World's Best-Loved Poems. New York: Avenel Books, 1931.